Algernon West

Sir Charles Wood's administration of Indian affairs from 1859 to 1866

Algernon West

Sir Charles Wood's administration of Indian affairs from 1859 to 1866

ISBN/EAN: 9783337305581

Printed in Europe, USA, Canada, Australia, Japan

Cover: Foto ©ninafisch / pixelio.de

More available books at **www.hansebooks.com**

SIR CHARLES WOOD'S

ADMINISTRATION OF

INDIAN AFFAIRS,

FROM 1859 TO 1866.

BY

ALGERNON WEST,

DEPUTY DIRECTOR OF INDIAN MILITARY FUNDS, AND LATELY
PRIVATE SECRETARY TO

THE RIGHT HON. SIR CHARLES WOOD, BART., M.P., G.C.B.,

AND

THE EARL DE GREY AND RIPON.

LONDON:
SMITH, ELDER AND CO., 65, CORNHILL.
1867.

TO THE

HEADS OF DEPARTMENTS IN THE INDIA OFFICE,

WHO HAVE HAD THE AMPLEST OPPORTUNITIES OF

OBSERVING THE BENEFICIAL EFFECT OF

Sir Charles Wood's Administration,

AND TO WHOSE UNOBTRUSIVE ASSISTANCE, AND UNSELFISH LABOURS,

NOT ONLY SUCCESSIVE SECRETARIES OF STATE, BUT THE

GOVERNMENT OF INDIA AND THE BRITISH NATION,

OWE A LASTING DEBT OF GRATITUDE—

THIS WORK IS DEDICATED.

As a monument of his ability, industry, and judgment, Sir Charles Wood may fairly point to his six years' administration of India, during a period of transition and unexampled difficulty at home and abroad. He found everything in disorder, and had everything to reconstruct.

He had to recast the whole judicial system of India—to create for her a paper currency—to superintend the remodelling of her taxation, and the reorganization of her finances. He had to develope a railway system, and last, and most difficult of all, to carry through the herculean labour of amalgamating the Queen's armies. If it has been impossible to do justice to every individual, we believe that, upon the whole, the Indian army has been a gainer under the change.

Where is the man possessed of that extent and variety of knowledge, that quickness, industry, and versatility, that acquaintance with matters financial, military, naval, judicial, and political, which will enable him to rule with a firm and unfaltering hand the mighty destinies of 150,000,000 of the human race?—*Times*, Feb. 6, 1866.

No tale in Hindoo mythology is more wonderful than the change which has been wrought in India within the last few years. The enchanters that have worked the spell have been peace, justice, and commerce. It may be added, that the system first fairly tried of governing India through a Secretary of State, directly and personally responsible to Parliament, has proved beyond expectation successful,—*Edinburgh Review*, July, 1864.

PREFACE.

I HOPE the statements contained in the following sketch will be found accurate.

If this merit be conceded to them, the credit will not be due to me, for, great as are the advantages which I have derived from the possession of all the private correspondence of Sir Charles Wood and Lord de Grey with the successive Governor-Generals and other high authorities in India, I feel that accuracy has only been rendered possible by the additions, revisions, and corrections of many friends in and out of the India Office, whose assistance has been freely given, not so much from motives of personal kindness to myself, as from the affection borne by them to their old chief, who, though now sitting in the House of Peers as Viscount Halifax, will ever be remembered in connection with India as Sir Charles Wood.

ALGERNON WEST.

India Office,
January 1, 1867.

CONTENTS.

CHAPTER I.
INTRODUCTION 1

CHAPTER II.
HOME GOVERNMENT 8

CHAPTER III.
GOVERNMENT OF INDIA AND PARLIAMENTARY LEGISLATION., ... 20

CHAPTER IV.
LAW AND JUSTICE 34

CHAPTER V.
INDIGO AND CONTRACT LAW, AND RENT 42

CHAPTER VI.
FINANCE 64

CHAPTER VII.
CURRENCY 89

CHAPTER VIII.
LAND REVENUE 100

CHAPTER IX.

Public Works 109

CHAPTER X.

Cotton 116

CHAPTER XI.

Education 126

CHAPTER XII.

Political 135

CHAPTER XIII.

Military 151

CHAPTER XIV.

Police 171

CHAPTER XV.

Navy 174

CHAPTER XVI.

Conclusion 177

SIR CHARLES WOOD'S

ADMINISTRATION OF

INDIAN AFFAIRS.

CHAPTER I.

INTRODUCTION.

It is proposed to show in the following pages, very briefly, the various acts of Sir Charles Wood's administration of India, from June, 1859, to the commencement of 1866.

The subjects with which he had to deal were numerous—the difficulties to be encountered were of no small magnitude. He had, in fact, to reconstruct the Government at home, and to place not only the Government of India, but every branch of its administration, upon such a footing as the experience of recent years and the requirements of modern times rendered necessary. The councils of the Governor-General and of the minor Presidencies, the courts of judicature, the civil service, the army, the navy, and the police, were all to be dealt with. The codification and administration of the law, the system of land revenue, the finance and the currency, demanded most careful consideration and vigorous action.

It would be impossible that all these questions, distinct as they are from one another, should be dealt with chronologically. They will all therefore be touched upon under separate chapters.

In order that the position of affairs when Sir Charles Wood entered upon office may be clearly understood, it is necessary that a short account should be given of the Parliamentary proceedings of 1858, which resulted in the transfer of the Government of India from the East India Company to the Crown.

The mind of the English people had scarcely recovered from the crushing effect of the first news of the outbreak at Meerut and the capture of Delhi, when a cry arose against the East India Company. Popular indignation, ever seeking a cause and demanding a victim for any national disaster, with some justice and much injustice, selected the Company as its victim, attributing to their neglect or mismanagement all the sorrows and sufferings of the Great Indian Mutiny.

Before the opening of the session of 1858, Lord Palmerston intimated to the Court of Directors the intention of her Majesty's Government to introduce a bill for the transfer of the authority and possessions of the East India Company to the Crown.

This communication called forth an able Memorandum of the improvements in the administration of India during the last thirty years, and a petition from the East India Company to Parliament, which, immediately on the assembling of the House of Lords, was presented by Lord Grey; and a debate ensued, in which the Duke of Argyll, without disclosing the measure of the Government, which was to be brought forward in the Lower House, justified the course about to be pursued by the ministry.

During the last century India had afforded subjects enough for trials of party strength, and for feats of oratorical display, among the giants of debate. The sparkling brilliancy of Sheridan, the commanding energy of Fox, the rounded periods of Pitt, the genius of Windham, the eloquence of Grey, the impassioned denunciations of Burke, had all been raised to the highest pitch in the stormy contest of Parliamentary strife engendered by Indian politics; but not for a long time had they so completely engrossed the attention of Parliament as they did at the commencement of 1858.

Lord Palmerston introduced his bill in a very different strain from the fierce attacks of Burke, who had asserted in his famous speech on Mr. Fox's bill of 1783, that "there is not a single prince, state, or " potentate, great or small, in India, with whom the " East India Company have come into contact, whom " they have not sold; that there is not a single treaty " they have ever made which they have not broken; " that there is not a single prince or state who ever " put any trust in the Company, who is not utterly " ruined."

Lord Palmerston approached the subject in a spirit of conciliation, "not of hostility, to the East India Com-

" pany, or as meaning to imply any blame or censure
" upon the administration of India under that corpora-
" tion." But he showed that its time was past, and that
the machinery of the double government was cumbrous
and out of date. He pointed out also that the East
India Company as an instrument of Government was
superfluous and irresponsible, and demonstrated the
advantage likely to ensue from the authority of the
Company being made over to the Crown, and the vast
importance of additional Parliamentary control and
responsibility that would be thus attained.

Sir George Lewis, in one of his ablest speeches,
insisted on this point :—" I do most confidently
" maintain," said he, " that no civilized Government
" ever existed on the face of this earth which was
" more corrupt, more perfidious, and more rapacious,
" than the Government of the East India Company
" was from 1758 to 1784, when it was placed under
" Parliamentary control."

The Bill proposed that there should be a President,
with a salary and position equal to that of a Secretary
of State, and a Council of eight, who were to be
nominated by the Crown, for eight years, two of them
retiring by rotation every two years.

In all matters but those of finance the President's
decision was to be final, the members of the Council,
should they differ from him, having the privilege of
recording their dissent. In matters entailing expenditure from the revenues of India, it was necessary that
the President should have the concurrence of at least
four members of his Council.

A majority of 145 in favour of the introduction of the Bill affirmed its principle; but, in a few days after the division, the Government was defeated on the Conspiracy Bill, and Lord Palmerston resigned.

He was succeeded by Lord Derby as Premier; and the new ministry, almost immediately on taking office, considered it advisable to introduce a bill for the better government of India, founded in a great measure on that of their predecessors.

In the second Bill it was proposed that there should be a Secretary of State, and a Council composed of eighteen members; nine were to be nominated by the Crown, and were mentioned by name in the Bill, and nine were to be elected. Four out of these last must have served her Majesty in India for ten years, or have been engaged in trade in that country for fifteen years, and were to be elected by the votes of any one in this country who had served her Majesty or the Government of India for ten years, or any proprietor of capital stock in Indian railways or other public work in India to the amount of 2,000*l.*, or any proprietor of India stock to the amount of 1,000*l.* The other five were to be possessed of the following qualification:—They must have been engaged in commerce in India, or in the exportation of manufactured articles to that country for five years, or must have resided there ten years. These latter were to be elected by the Parliamentary constituencies of London, Manchester, Liverpool, Glasgow, and Belfast.

This Bill, however, found no support, either in the

House, or in the country, and was withdrawn without having reached a second reading.

On Lord John Russell's suggestion, resolutions were proposed in a committee of the whole House, and, after many nights of discussion, and many amendments, a Bill was at last framed in accordance with the resolutions as passed by the House.

A new Secretary of State was created, to whom, aided by a council of fifteen members, was entrusted the home government of India. Of the first fifteen, seven were to be elected from among the existing or late Directors of the East India Company by the Court of Directors, and eight were to be nominated by the Crown. The majority of persons so elected or nominated were to have resided or served in India for ten years, and, excepting in the case of late and present Directors, and officers on the Home Establishment of the East India Company, who had so served, or resided, they were not to have left India for more than ten years preceding the date of their appointment. The Council were to meet once in every week, when they were to be presided over by the Secretary of State, or, in his absence, by a Vice-President appointed by him. Questions were to be determined in Council by the vote of the majority, but, except on any matter involving expenditure from the revenues of India, and in some cases of patronage, the Secretary of State might over-rule the decision of the majority.

In all cases of disagreement, the Secretary of State or any member of the Council might record his opinion.

The Secretary of State had the further power of sending orders without the concurrence of his council, but in these cases the orders were to lie on the table for seven days, and every member of Council might state his views in writing; and, if those of the majority were opposed to the course adopted by the Secretary of State, he was bound to place his reasons on record.

The Act did not come into operation till the autumn of the year 1858, and for the remainder of the time in which Lord Derby's Government was in power Lord Stanley held the seals of Secretary of State for the India Department; but his tenure of office was short.

CHAPTER II.

HOME GOVERNMENT.

ON the formation of Lord Palmerston's Government, in June, 1859, Sir Charles Wood accepted the post of Secretary of State for India. His last office had been that of First Lord of the Admiralty, but it was only four years and a half since he had, as President of the Board of Control, taken a leading part in the Home Government of India.

In that short interval a complete change in the form of the Home Government had been effected. The grand old East India Company, with all its prestige and all its associations, which had held sway for a hundred years over India, had, as has been shown, been swept away, and its authority transferred to the Crown. Instead of a President of the Board of Control, sitting in Cannon Row, and the Court of Directors of the East India Company, in Leadenhall Street, there was now a Secretary of State, with a Council.

There can be no question of the great advantage of giving to the Secretary of State for India the aid of a Council composed of persons experienced in one branch or another of Indian administration, and no one felt this more strongly, or could be more disposed to avail himself of their assistance, than Sir Charles Wood. It must not be forgotten that in the India Office is concentrated the collective business, not merely of a department, but of an empire: finance, currency, legislation, revenue, foreign policy, army, public works—all require the consideration and decision of the minister occupying the position of Secretary of State for India; but no man, however experienced and laborious, could properly direct and control the various interests of so vast an empire, unless he were aided, as Sir Charles Wood was, by men with knowledge of different parts of the country, and possessing an intimate acquaintance with the difficult and complicated subjects involved in the government and welfare of so many incongruous races.

The selection of Councillors had been made with great judgment, and consisted of men of tried ability in various departments, but many of them had no previous experience of the mode of conducting business in England. The official staff consisted of men selected partly from the officers of the old East India House, and partly from those of the Board of Control. It is superfluous to say anything of the merits of a service which has been so justly celebrated, from the time of Charles Lamb, James Mill, his yet more distinguished son, John Stuart Mill, Sir James Melvill, Mr. Hawkins, and Mr. Waterfield, to the present day, when it counts among its ranks the accomplished historian of Affghanistan and the Sepoy war, and many men whose financial, legal, and literary reputations have far out-reached the narrow limits of a Government Office. Practically, however, the working of the department in its new form of a Secretary of State's office, with a Council and an establishment nominally consolidated from those of Leadenhall Street and Cannon Row, was inharmonious and crude, and the whole procedure of official business had still to be adapted to the new order of things.

Although there were, therefore, ample materials of the best quality at the command of the Secretary of State for conducting the business even of so extensive a territory as our Indian Empire, it needed the power and organization of a master-mind to arrange these materials in such a manner as to turn them to the best account, and this was the first task which Sir Charles Wood had to encounter.

In order to give an accurate idea of the official difficulties which attended the change of Government from the East India Company and Board of Control to a Secretary of State in Council, it will be necessary to show the order of business that existed under the former system. The initiation of despatches on all subjects rested with the heads of departments in the East India House, either under the instructions or subject to the approval of the chairman and deputy chairman; the drafts of despatches, technically termed previous communications, were then submitted by the "Chairs" to the President of the Board of Control, who made such alterations as he thought necessary, and returned them to the "Chairs," by whom they were then sent to one or other of the three committees; when passed by that committee, they were laid before the full court, and, when sanctioned by them, were officially forwarded for the final approval of the Board.

When Sir Charles Wood took office, he found the Council divided into three committees, in nearly the same manner as the Court of Directors of the East India Company had been. The despatches were prepared by the Secretaries of the Department, as in the old India House, but instead of being brought in any way before the Secretary of State, they were sent directly to one of the committees, and only reached the eye of the Secretary of State when the members of that committee were pledged to the views which they had already approved.

It is obvious that this mode of conducting the business was not only inconsistent with the principle of the Secretary of State's directing the policy, but actually placed him in a worse position than the President of the Board of Control; whereas there can be no doubt that the great object of the change in the constitution of the Home Department of the India Government was to increase the power and responsibility of its chief, who was for that purpose created a Secretary of State. It is true that, unlike other Secretaries of State, a council was added to assist him with their advice, and supply local Indian experience, but on the Secretary of State rested the responsibility, and with the responsibility the power. "The minister," said Lord Stanley, "is bound to hear the advice given " by his council, but he is not bound to take it. It is "for him to decide whether he will take or reject it; "and, whether he takes or rejects it, he will equally "act upon his own responsibility."

Sir Charles Wood at once discerned this very serious defect in the mode of business, and took immediate steps to remedy it by assuming to himself the initiatory power, and placing the office, as had been intended, on the usual footing of that of a Secretary of State, his Council taking their proper position as his advisers. He divided the Council into six committees, of five members each, every member being on two committees, the chairman being selected by the Secretary of State. The drafts of the despatches were prepared, as before, by the secretary of the department, and when seen by one of the under-secretaries, were submitted to the Secretary of State, who, after making such alterations as he thought fit, referred them to one of the committees. The draft, as considered and amended, if necessary, by the committee, was returned to the Secretary of State, and by him sent to Council in such shape as he might determine for final consideration and decision.

In addition to this alteration in the system of business, the arrangement of departments in the India Office was generally revised. The military and marine branches had hitherto been distinct from the general correspondence department, to the duties of which the work of those branches was analogous, and to which they were now united.

The system of account, pay, and audit was cumbrous and expensive, and, at the same time, inefficient;

for although there was an accountant-general, a cashier, and an auditor, exclusive of the auditor appointed under the Act for the better government of India (General Jameson), with a separate staff to each, there was no adequate check on expenditure, nor any sufficient examination of accounts. By the combination of the three departments under the accountant-general, a more efficient and economical system was introduced; the *final* audit, which has been, and is, completely satisfactory, being entrusted to General Jameson.

In the Store Department, where a complete revision was made of the manner by which stores were supplied to the various Governments in India, the system which had been continued from the trading days of the East India Company was found to be defective in many respects, and especially in the absence of direct responsibility on the part of any one person. It was, accordingly, determined to place the supply of stores on a footing which, while insuring a more perfect responsibility, should be thoroughly efficient to meet the rapidly increasing requirements of our great Eastern dependency.

With this view a department was constituted, under a Director-General, who was to represent the Secretary of State in Council in regard to all contracts with the public, and in whom was to be vested the general responsibility for the supply, examination, and shipment of all stores. To assist him in the latter branches of the business, an Inspector of stores was appointed, subordinate to him; and, this post being held by an officer of great professional experience, who is aided by a competent staff of assistants possessing the requisite technical acquirements, the utmost efficiency has been secured.

Except in the case of articles of a special nature, or those of which the supply is limited to a few large firms, it was decided to adopt the system of open competition, and to invite tenders by public advertisement.

The great importance of this question is evident when it is considered that stores of all kinds, whether military, ordnance, clothing, medical, stationery, mint, telegraph, or public works, are annually despatched for the use of the several presidencies, to the value of about a million sterling.

In these and all other arrangements Sir Charles Wood was materially assisted by Mr. Baring, formerly his private secretary at the Board of Control, whose talent for organization was of especial advantage in the re-arrangement of the department, and who, from his peculiar aptitude for business, his power of work, and the experience he had acquired from having been employed in various public departments, had attained a degree of official knowledge unequalled by any of his contemporaries in the House of Commons. The unpopularity incidental to any measure necessitating alteration and reduction in a Government office was, in this instance, to a great extent overcome from its being apparent that the improvements were carried out, not from a love of change, but for the good of the service, and in strict accordance with justice. It will be long before this merit in Mr. Baring ceases to be recognized in the India Office. He had not, however, the opportunity of watching the practical workings of those reforms, in the introduction of which he had borne so prominent a part.

Mr. Sidney Herbert's elevation to the peerage rendered it necessary that the War Office should be represented in the House of Commons, and, in order to attain this object, Mr. Baring was transferred to that department. This appointment was amply justified by the able manner in which, with very short time for preparation, he mastered the complicated details of the army estimates, and carried them through the House of Commons. The popularity which Lord de Grey had acquired in the organization of the Volunteer Force at the War Department, was a guarantee that the military changes then in progress in our Eastern Empire would not suffer by his removal to the India Office. The lamented death of Lord Herbert, however, in the prime of his intellectual vigour, and the appointment of Sir George Lewis as his successor, led to the re-transfer of these two Under Secretaries in the summer of 1861. Two years had not elapsed, before the retirement of Mr. Lowe from the Council of Education, and Mr. Henry Austen Bruce's appointment in his place, left a new field of usefulness open for Mr. Baring at the Home Office, and the Government was strengthened by the acquisition of Lord Wodehouse as Under Secretary for India.

The political exigencies of Parliament were not

the sole causes which led to rapid changes in the India Office. The illness and consequent resignation of the Earl of Carlisle, the Lord Lieutenant of Ireland, removed Lord Wodehouse, in 1864, to a higher position, where his firmness and decision of character were eminently displayed in grappling with the discontent and agitation of that unhappy country. Once more the Ministerial ranks were reinforced, by the addition of Lord Dufferin, who, formerly known as a daring yachtsman, and a graceful writer, and subsequently as an able diplomatist in Syria, has by his lucid speeches on the vexed questions of the Indian Army, and land tenure in Ireland, raised yet higher the hopes entertained of the distinguished career that in all probability awaits him.

These constantly recurring changes diminished, to a great extent, the practical advantage which the Secretary of State would otherwise have derived from the undoubted abilities of his Parliamentary Under Secretaries; for scarcely were they enabled to master the rudiments of Indian government, when their services were transferred to some other department. Indeed, the position of the Under Secretaries of State for India has never been on a proper footing.

In the same relation as other Under Secretaries of State to their chief, they had no recognized place in the Council, and were unable to take any part in the deliberations of that body. Sir Charles Wood did all in his power to remedy this anomaly, by causing all papers to be referred to them, and arranging that one of the Under Secretaries should always attend the periodical meetings of Council, so that he might have an opportunity of at least hearing their discussions : but this, it must be admitted, is scarcely a fitting position for the Under Secretary of State who would have to defend, either in the House of Lords or House of Commons, the policy of the Home Government.

It was well, therefore, for Sir Charles Wood that, in his permanent Council, he found not only experienced advice, but most ready assistance, of which he gladly and largely availed himself. Not satisfied with the mere formal reference of documents to the committees, it was his constant practice to consult his councillors individually, and to invite them to state their opinions freely. Very few days ever elapsed without his seeing many of the members of Council. The chairmen of the committees were requested to confer with him on papers awaiting their consideration; and, in matters of more than ordinary difficulty, he would himself attend the committees and personally take part in their discussion. To this friendly communication, no doubt, is in a great measure due the smoothing down of many difficulties, and removal of many stumbling-blocks from the path, which might have caused trouble, if opinions had been placed on record in a full committee, before an opportunity occurred for the discussion and interchange of ideas on the subject with the Secretary of State.

It has never been imputed to Sir Charles Wood that he is wanting in self-reliance, or that he is too easily led by the opinion of others. It is, therefore, a convincing testimony to the skill and tact with which he availed himself of the abilities and experience of the members of his Council, and of the practical utility of the mode of transacting the business which he introduced, that, during his whole tenure of office, Sir Charles Wood overruled them only four times, on all of which occasions subjects of minor importance only were involved.

With these few exceptions, and the larger and imperial question of the discontinuance of a local European army, to which reference will be made hereafter, Sir Charles Wood has carried with him the majority of his Council on all the varied measures which were inaugurated and executed at home and in India. Indeed, so complete was the agreement between them, that, in the House of Lords, in the session of 1863, a complaint was made " that " they never heard of what the Council of India " did—occasionally there was a dissent, and nothing " more." The names of Sir John Lawrence, Sir George Clerk, and many others are sufficient evidence that this unanimity was not the result of any lack of independence on the part of the Council, but was a proof of their earnest and willing co-operation with a Secretary of State, whose far-sighted views were fully appreciated and perceived by them to be advantageous to the great interests entrusted to their charge.

One of the main features of the success of Sir Charles Wood's administration, was the constant personal communication he held, not only with his Councillors, and with the members of the India Office secretariat, but with others unconnected with the department. No man ever came from India, whatever his position, with information likely to be of use to the public service, but found easy access to the private ear of the Secretary of State. Quick, and somewhat intolerant as he was of those lengthy narratives of purely personal interest often attempted to be placed before him, and which he keenly felt did but waste the time due to more important business, no man ever bestowed a more impartial or patient hearing on those whose experience or knowledge entitled them to attention. Many were those who, on leaving his room after one of these interviews, expressed their astonishment at the perfect intimacy he displayed with matters supposed by them to be technical, or only to be attained after a long residence in India, and by years of application to a particular subject.

CHAPTER III.

GOVERNMENT OF INDIA AND PARLIAMENTARY LEGISLATION.

WHILE changes in Indian affairs had occurred rapidly at home, how was it in the East, since Sir Charles Wood had ceased to be president of the Board of Control four short years ago?

In that infinitesimal period of a country's history, what a wonderful alteration had taken place in India itself! The little cloud on the horizon, spoken of by Lord Canning before taking his departure from England, had not then arisen. India, it was hoped, had entered upon an era of peace and advancement which was to be undisturbed by aggression or aggrandizement. The whole empire was in a state of tranquillity; the revenue was flourishing, and it might well have been anticipated that the only coming task of the Government would be the development of the resources of the country, the education of the people, the improved administration of justice, and the prosecution of public works. But now it had come to pass that the heaven was black with cloud and wind, the mutiny had passed over the land, marking its fiery course in bloodshed, ruin, and confusion.

The finances were disordered, confidence was destroyed, a flourishing condition of revenue had changed into a chronic state of yearly deficits and loans. The Sepoy army, hitherto blindly trusted and beloved, had been dissolved, and the conduct of the East India Company's European troops had verged on mutiny.

It was not unnatural, when all men's energies had been strained to the uttermost by the exciting scenes of the mutiny, that there should follow a period of inaction; and the *Friend of India* observed that " the events of the year 1859 might best be " expressed in negatives; nothing has been done for " public works, and nothing for education. The police " has not been reformed, a road system has not been " organized, civilization has not advanced, and the " administration has not improved."

Lord Stanley's tenure of office, though long enough to show that in him ability and statesmanship were joined to great application, and a yet greater interest in the affairs of India, had been too short to enable him to carry out great reforms in the administration.

The session of 1860, so far as regarded Indian affairs, was fully occupied with the pressing questions connected with the change in the European forces and Native army of India; but in the session of 1861 Sir Charles Wood introduced into Parliament three bills, all deeply affecting the welfare of India. These three measures were all carried with but little discussion, and with no opposition worthy of the name.

The first of these bills was to make better provision

for the constitution of the Council of the Governor-General, and the local government of the several presidencies and provinces of India, so as to render the legislative authority more suited to the requirements of the times, and to the altered state of circumstances in that country.

It is unnecessary to refer to earlier days, but from 1833 to 1861 legislative enactments for all India had their origin and their completion with the Governor-General in Council at Calcutta. The minor Presidencies of Madras and Bombay were powerless to make a law on the most trivial subject affecting their own local interests.

With regard to the Council of the Governor-General, the Act of 1833 had added to it a member appointed from England, whose presence was necessary for the passing of any legislative enactment required for any part of British India. This constitution of the central legislative body lasted up to 1853, when members of the Civil Service from each Presidency and Lieutenant-Governorship, as well as two of the judges of the Supreme Court, were added, in accordance with the provisions of a bill which was introduced into Parliament by Sir Charles Wood, at that time President of the Board of Control, for the purpose of gaining their experience of the varying conditions, habits, and requirements of the people, and of giving material assistance in the then increasing labours of the Council. The working, however, of this Council was not found to be altogether satisfactory; Lord Canning was most anxious to see it placed on a better footing, and pointed out its defects, as well as the general nature of the improvements which were desired in India.

The English settlers were anxious to be represented in a Calcutta Parliament, but, as has been well said in the *Edinburgh Review*, "A Calcutta legis-
" lature would be the legislature of a class in its worst
" and most aggravated form. The public opinion of
" India is virtually the opinion of the small but
" powerful European community; its interests are
" mainly commercial, and its ideas of policy and of
" law are liable to the bias and insuperable tempta-
" tions which commercial interests involve."

In the opinion of Sir Charles Wood, a claim to a place in the body by which laws for all India were to be passed, equally strong with that of the English settlers, existed on the part of the natives of India. By the legislation of the Governor-General's Council the interests of millions of the native population were affected, and, however well acquainted with them might be those members of the Civil Service who had passed great part of their lives in the provinces, it could not be but that natives should still more faithfully represent their interests and wishes.

Sir Charles Wood was deeply impressed with the importance of the subject, and was also anxious to have the advantage of Lord Canning's services in carrying out the alterations of the Council, as his thorough knowledge of the question rendered him by far the fittest man for completing so desirable a change. As soon, therefore, as he was fully in pos-

of Bengal, and the ordinary members of Council, a civil servant recommended by the Governor of each of the Presidencies, together with three native noblemen, and two gentlemen selected from among the commercial classes of Calcutta.

Authority was given for the Council of the Governor-General to meet in any place within the territories of India to which it might be summoned by him; and the first Council held out of Calcutta assembled at Simla in 1862.

The Governor-General was also authorized to make rules and orders from time to time for the guidance of his Council, and, in consequence of the arrangements made, a system of departmental responsibility has sprung up, which has greatly improved and facilitated the despatch of business by the chief executive Government in India. It has, however, been carefully kept in view, that there should be nothing in the measure to detract from the supreme authority of the Viceroy and his Council; indeed a new and extraordinary power was conferred on the Governor-General, of making and promulgating ordinances, in cases of emergency, on his own responsibility.

Councils of a somewhat similar constitution were created in Madras, Bombay, and Bengal, to which non-official Europeans and natives were to be admitted.

On any questions connected with the debt, the customs, the army, and other matters affecting the whole empire, the local legislatures were prohibited from entering, without the previous sanction of the Governor-General; but they were empowered to legislate on all internal matters peculiar to their own Presidencies.

The authorities in Madras and Bombay were not backward in availing themselves of the power of admitting natives conferred on them by the Act. A native gentleman was immediately appointed to the Council in Madras; and in Bombay, Sir George Clerk selected for this high honour no less than four, whose usefulness in Council fully justified the confidence he had reposed in them.

One other provision in this Act must not be unnoticed, and that is the succession to the office of Governor-General, in the event of a vacancy happening when no one in India had been provisionally appointed to that office. Previously to this Act, the senior member of Council assumed the post of Governor-General on the occurrence of an unexpected vacancy, but now the Governor of Madras or Bombay, whichever of the two might happen to be the senior in date of appointment, would, as a matter of course, act as Governor-General in such circumstances.

The next step in legislating for India, at home, was taken by the introduction of a bill for establishing High Courts of Judicature in India. The idea had been long contemplated of substituting for the Supreme and Sudder Court, a single court, which should combine the legal power and authority of the former, with the intimate knowledge of the customs and of the natives of the country possessed by the judges of the latter, and should exercise jurisdiction both over the provinces which had been under the Sudder Courts, and over the Presidency towns in which the Supreme Court had entire local jurisdiction.

Before these Courts were formed, if an Englishman, at whatever distance from the Presidency town, was accused of a crime, it was necessary that he should be brought down with all the witnesses to Calcutta ; and it cannot be denied that the inconvenience and expense of such a course frustrated the ends of justice in a large number of cases. This has now been remedied by the power given in the Act for trying Europeans elsewhere than in the Presidency towns.

The new law gave authority for the formation of High Courts by the issue of letters patent under the great seal, and accordingly they were, in 1862, constituted in all the Presidency towns; and later, in 1866, a similar course was pursued in establishing a High Court for the North-Western Provinces.

A native judge now sits on the bench of the High Court of Calcutta, with great honour to himself and advantage to the administration of law ; and, with such a prospect of advancement, it may be confidently hoped that other native gentlemen will in time qualify themselves for similar high positions of responsibility.

It was a matter of no slight difficulty to amalgamate the Supreme and Sudder Courts, and to bring the judges, so dissimilar in every respect in their education and training, to work harmoniously together.

The greatest credit is due to the Chief Justice, Sir Barnes Peacock, for the hearty way in which he worked to overcome these difficulties; and the success that has signally attended the measure in Calcutta is in a great degree owing to his exertion, zeal, and discretion.

The third measure introduced into Parliament during this session was the Civil Service Bill, which, in the first instance, rendered valid nominations to certain appointments which, it was stated, had been made by the local government, in violation of the law requiring that they should be filled by members of the Covenanted Civil Service only. The number of that service had for some years been found inadequate to supply the demands upon it; and the practice of appointing to important posts, contrary to the letter of the law, gentlemen who were not members of the Civil Service, had largely increased in the non-regulation provinces, as they were termed, which the great extension of the British empire during the administration of Lord Dalhousie brought under our rule. It was incumbent on the Government to provide a remedy for such a state of things as soon as it was brought to their notice.

After the necessary provisions for this purpose, the Act proceeds to declare what offices shall ordinarily be held by members of the Civil Service, provision being made for appointing other than civil servants to such offices under special circumstances, subject to the approval of the Secretary of State in Council, to whom the appointment is immediately to be reported.

The Act, though objected to in the first instance by the Council of India, was ultimately passed with general approval, and many posts of considerable importance have been thus thrown open to persons not in the Civil Service. An instance of its working has been shown in the appointment, by Lord Canning, of a military officer, Colonel Durand, to the high position of Foreign Secretary, his peculiar qualifications and fitness for the place being a valid justification for the departure from ordinary rules.

This appointment, the nomination of the new councillors, and the arrangements for the business of his Council, were among the last acts of Lord Canning's administration. At the time, indeed, when these measures were under consideration, his period of office was fast drawing to an honourable close; but Sir Charles Wood felt of what paramount importance it was that he should remain for a time to carry out at least some of the many wise and beneficial measures already initiated by him. It was fitting that to him, rather than to any other, it should be given to inaugurate a new policy in new circumstances; and, as to him belonged the priceless honour of having conducted with a firm yet merciful hand the government of the country through the sore trial of the mutiny, so it was right that to him should also belong the honour of pacification and reconstruction.

Ever ready to postpone his own wishes to the public good, he determined to remain for one year more—that fatal one year more, which sent him home, as it had sent Lord Dalhousie home, with his health ruined, and constitution shattered, by the cares and anxieties of his eventful viceroyalty. Lord Canning's departure from the scene of his great achievements, when it did come, was a matter of deep sorrow to all in India. His calm demeanour and steadfast perseverance in the path which he had marked out for his conduct in India, no less than the series of great measures which he had set on foot for the benefit of the people, had long ago silenced those (and they had been not a few) who, themselves overpowered by the events of the mutiny, had not minds sufficiently enlarged to admire and respect the man, who, amidst their fears and terrors, had calmly stood his ground, and had dealt justice fearlessly and unshrinkingly to all, little heeding their petty jeers and their paltry clamour, and earning for himself the name of "Clemency Canning," which, instead of being a byword of reproach, will for ever entitle him to respect and admiration.

That after Lord Canning it would be difficult to obtain a fitting successor to occupy his post, was only too obvious. At the close of 1861, however, it became necessary for Sir Charles Wood to recommend a new Governor-General to the Queen, and his choice fell on the Earl of Elgin, who had already had large experience, in various capacities, in most quarters of the globe. After a brilliant career at Oxford, he had commenced his public services as Governor of Jamaica. He was subsequently appointed to the Governor-Generalship of Canada, where he remained eight years, and concluded the well-known treaty of reciprocity between the United States and the North American Colonies, which has produced so much advantage to those countries. His two expeditions to China, and his treaties of Tientsin and Jeddo, evinced in him a singular combination of firmness and conciliation; but it must have been with feelings of heavy responsibility that he assumed an office so important as that of Governor-General of India.

How he might have performed such high duties, what might have been his policy, what his ultimate success, it has not been given to us to know; for, after a short viceroyalty, he was seized with a mortal illness, whilst traversing the Himalayas at a point 13,000 feet above the sea, from which he never rallied. It was towards the end of November, 1863, that the news of his illness and resignation reached London, too soon followed by the intelligence of his death. Again the responsibility of selecting a Governor-General devolved on Sir Charles Wood. The circumstances of India at the time rendered it desirable that no delay should occur in filling up the appointment, and, within three days of receiving the intelligence of Lord Elgin's death, Sir Charles Wood submitted the name of his successor to the Queen. At that time, hard at work at his post in the India Office, sat the man who of all men was pre-eminently entitled from his past services to claim at the hands of the ministers the office of Governor-General of India. No claim, no request, ever came from Sir John Lawrence. With the modesty always characteristic of true greatness, he did not even suspect that the vacant appointment would be offered to him; but, when the Queen's commands were conveyed to him by Sir Charles Wood, unexpected as they were, they did not deprive him of his ready power of decision, for, before leaving the room, he had virtually undertaken the weighty cares and responsibilities of the government of the greatest country under British rule, the most important office that can be offered by any Government to any man.

In recording the rapid succession of Governor-Generals, it is impossible to avoid glancing at the havoc which has been made by death among the great men with whom Sir Charles Wood's administration of India was associated.

Three of the foremost returned only to die in England, and to receive all that their grateful country could offer to her most distinguished sons, as a tribute of her gratitude and admiration. Thrice during seven years have the lofty gates of our old Abbey opened to receive the remains of Indian statesmen and soldiers; Lord Canning, Sir James Outram, and Lord Clyde, who in life were joined in one common struggle and endeavour to maintain our power in India, in death are united in the holy fellowship of one common resting-place. But these are not all on whom the hand of death has fallen: Lord Elgin, buried in the picturesque little village of Durmsala in the Himalayas; Lord Elphinstone, whose able governorship of Bombay was productive of the most happy results to that Presidency, and pointed him out, had he been spared, as the successor to Lord Canning; Sir Henry Ward, who, during the few months he governed Madras, well maintained in India the reputation gained in the Ionian Islands and Ceylon, of an able administrator and loyal servant of the

Crown,—all played a conspicuous part in the history of their own country and of India.

Time would fail to tell of all who, though of lower rank and less prominent position, were not less earnest in walking the path of their appointed duties, or less ready to yield up their lives in the discharge of their allotted task.

The chasms, however, which were thus made by death in the ranks of Indian administrators, were worthily filled by those on whom the choice of the Home Government fell.

On Sir Henry Ward's death, Sir William Denison was transferred from the colony of New South Wales, which he had ably ruled for eight years, to the government of Madras, for the superintendence of the important public works in which Presidency his professional knowledge as an engineer pointed him out as being especially fitted. The appointments to Bombay of Sir George Clerk and of his successor, Sir Bartle Frere, were successful beyond all question; and their subsequent nomination to the Council of India at home, one by a Whig, and one by a Tory, Secretary of State, show how well their services have been appreciated in England.

CHAPTER IV.

LAW AND JUSTICE.

ONE of the greatest blessings conferred on the people of India in recent years has been the codification of the criminal law, and of the procedure, civil and criminal, of the courts of justice.

So long ago as 1833, a commission, of which the late Lord Macaulay was the first president, commenced at Calcutta the arduous task of compiling a penal code for India. This code was prepared in 1837, but did not assume the form of an enactment until 1860, when it was passed by the Legislative Council, and is now, as the Indian Penal Code, in active and successful operation throughout all the British possessions in India.

Another commission was appointed, for the purpose of revising the laws of India, by Sir Charles Wood, when he was President of the Board of Control in 1853, which brought to bear on the subject the professional knowledge of such men as Sir John Jervis, Lord Romilly, Sir Edward Ryan, Mr. Lowe, and Mr. Flower Ellis, and the practical and intimate acquaintance with the customs and laws of India, which was possessed by Mr. Cameron, Mr. Macleod, and Mr. Hawkins.

By this commission were prepared the admirable codes of civil and criminal procedure, which, substituting, as they did, simplicity and expedition for the complicated forms of pleading which had hitherto existed in the courts of India, became law in 1859 and 1861 respectively, and may now be said to be in force throughout nearly the whole of India.

In most of the non-regulation districts, and in Bengal, including the North-Western Provinces, their introduction has been attended with marked success; and the Lieutenant-Governor of Bengal has reported the prevailing opinion on the merits of the civil code in the following words:—" The result of all " the inquiries I have made of the native judges, " by whom nearly all original suits are tried, and " of whom I have now seen many, in different parts " of the Lower Provinces, is that the new procedure " in working has been successful even above all " hope ; " while the Lieutenant-Governor of the North-West Provinces affirms the measure to have " been one of the best that has ever been passed " by the legislature."

In 1861 Sir Charles Wood appointed another commission to prepare a code of civil law for India. Although mainly composed of the same members as the commission of 1853, it was strengthened by the addition of two of the most able judges of the land, Sir William Erle and Sir James Willes. The first part of this code has been embodied in Act X. of 1865, and comprises the law of succession and inheritance generally applicable to all classes domiciled in British India, other than Hindoo and Mahomedan, each of which portion of the community has laws of its own on such subjects.

An Act has recently been passed in India, giving a law of succession to the wealthy community of Parsees, who reside chiefly in Bombay, and who were previously subject to the law, very distasteful to them, administered by the Supreme Court, in matters of succession.

Small Cause Courts, with a simple procedure, have existed for many years within the limits of the presidency towns; but until recently no such courts had been established in the provinces. There, every case, of the most simple kind and of the smallest importance, was tried under a lengthy and complicated form of procedure, the tendency of which, by the obstacles it interposed in the way of a speedy decision, was to promote litigation, and to lead to a contest in many cases in which, under other circumstances, there would have been no contest at all. To add to the difficulties of obtaining prompt justice under such a system, every decision of every court was subject to appeal to a higher court, and in some cases to a second or special appeal to the highest court of all, the right of appeal being considered the great security for the efficient administration of justice by the subordinate tribunals. In 1860 an Act was passed by the Government of India for the establishment of courts in the provinces " with a view to the more " easy recovery of small debts and demands." These courts, instituted by the executive Government at places where they might be considered necessary, were to exercise jurisdiction to the extent of 50*l.*, and were required to conduct their proceedings according to the new code of civil procedure, to which reference has already been made. They were to be presided over by competent native or European judges, selected by the Government from among persons of judicial attainments, whether in or out of the service of Government, and their decisions were to be final, with the power of granting immediate execution, on the verbal application of the party in whose favour the decree was passed. On the same day an Act was passed abolishing the right of special appeal in any suit of a nature cognizable in Courts of Small Causes, when brought in any other court than a Small Cause Court. The working of the Small Cause Courts was carefully watched; measures were promptly taken for supplying omissions discovered in the legislative provisions under which they were originally constituted; and in 1865 an Act was passed, consolidating and amending the law relating to Small Cause Courts in the provinces. By this Act power was given to the local government to extend the jurisdiction of Small Cause Courts to 100*l.*, and to invest any person, for a limited period, with the powers of a judge of a Small Cause Court. In other respects the principles and rules applicable to these courts on their first establishment were strictly followed. Under the foregoing provisions, Small Cause Courts have been established in various places in the several presidencies of India, in the Punjab, and Scinde; and they have been very successful in disposing promptly and satisfactorily of much of that portion of the litigation of the country which relates to small debts and demands. In 1864 the jurisdiction of the Small Cause Courts within the limits of the presidency towns was raised from 50*l.* to 100*l.*, thus greatly increasing the usefulness of those courts.

At the ports of Rangoon, in Pegu, and Moulmein and Akyab, on the Tenasserim coast, which now form part of the jurisdiction of the Chief Commissioner of Burmah, Englishmen have settled in considerable numbers, and an extensive trade is being carried on, bringing into the European markets the various productions of that fertile territory. For the protection of the increasing trade at the ports above mentioned, an Act was passed by the Government of India, under the instruction of the Home Government, for the establishment of Recorders' Courts, to be presided over by a barrister, with full powers of civil and criminal jurisdiction, with the exception of the power to try European British subjects charged with capital offences, the High Court of Calcutta alone having power to try such cases. Provision was at the same time made for the establishment of Small Cause Courts in those places.

The Act for establishing Recorders' Courts in British Burmah was followed in 1865 by an Act for creating a Chief Court of Judicature in the Punjab and its dependencies. Thenceforth this court was to consist of two or more judges, one of whom at least must always be a barrister of not less than five years' standing. It was, like the High Courts within the limits of the presidencies, to be the ultimate court of appeal from the civil and criminal courts under its jurisdiction; and it was invested with original jurisdiction in any suit falling within the jurisdiction of any of its subordinate courts which it might think proper to try and determine as a court of first instance, and with full criminal jurisdiction over European British subjects as well as natives.

By an Act passed on the 21st of March, 1865, grand juries were abolished, and provision was made for the issue of commissions addressed by the Government to any of the judges of the High Court, authorizing them to hold sittings in such place, or places, as the Government might think expedient for the exercise of the original jurisdiction, criminal or civil, of the High Court. It was further provided that, in cases tried under such commissions, a majority of not less than nine out of the twelve jurors, with the concurrence of the presiding judge, should be competent to pronounce a verdict of guilty.

Legislative measures on many other important subjects were passed by the Government of India during the period under review. The results of those to which reference has been made above are, that an excellent penal code has been substituted for the old regulations on criminal law to be found in the numerous volumes containing the effects of previous legislation; that every person domiciled, or permanently settled in India, has now a law of inheritance and succession to which he can look for guidance in these important matters, while the fundamental rule of administering their own laws in such cases, to the Hindoo and Mahomedan subjects of the Crown in India, has been strictly adhered to; that almost the entire administration of civil and criminal justice in the British possessions in India is now under the supervision and control of trained judges, whereas, in 1860, no such judge could exercise jurisdiction in any of the proceedings of the provincial courts; that, whereas a European British subject could previously be tried only by the Supreme Court at the presidency town, he may now be tried at any place, nearest to that of the commission of his crime, at which a jury can be brought together; and that the proceedings of the courts, civil and criminal, are now regulated by codes of procedure vastly superior to those which preceded them. It may be said, without exaggeration, that no such progress has been made in improving the judicial administration of British India at any period, or, indeed, during the whole of the period, since the date of the Cornwallis code, as within the last seven years.

Most of these reforms in the administration of the law first assumed a definite shape in the form of bills laid before the Council of the Governor-General; but they had always been previously discussed, and to a certain degree determined upon, in private communication between Sir Charles Wood and Mr. Maine, the legislative member of Council, and Mr. Hawkins, the secretary of the Judicial Department in the India Office at home.

It was impossible that two men could be better qualified to give advice on such subjects.

Mr. Maine had early distinguished himself, as the most elegant scholar of his day, at Cambridge, where he was head of the classical tripos in 1845. Shortly after taking his degree he became Regius Professor of Civil Law, which appointment he retained until elected Reader in Roman Law and Jurisprudence at the Middle Temple. His comprehensive work on ancient law, and other writings, added largely to his reputation in this country; and his appointment to the Council of the Governor-General in India has afforded him a fitting, and an ample, field for the exercise of all his powers.

To a familiar acquaintance with the habits and customs of the people of India, acquired during a residence of twenty-seven years in that country, Mr. Hawkins added a deep and intimate knowledge of Indian law and the ripe experience of an official life. Originally a member of the Civil Service, he had occupied, for ten years, the important post of Registrar of the Sudder Court of Calcutta, and two years that of Judge of the Court.

In 1853 he was appointed a member of the Indian Law Commission, and in 1854 became its secretary. In 1856 the Court of Directors, ever happy in its selection of their public servants, appointed him to the judicial and legislative department of the East India House, from which he was, to the regret of all who knew him, compelled by illness to retire at the commencement of 1866.

CHAPTER V.

INDIGO AND CONTRACT LAW, AND RENT.

Out of an attempt to alter one of the provisions of the Penal Code, as to the description of breaches of contract which was to be dealt with as criminal, arose a question which convulsed society in Bengal to its centre, and was discussed with much violence and acrimony soon after Sir Charles Wood's accession to office. For the better understanding of the wise and consistent course pursued by him in this matter, it will be necessary to advert briefly to the situation in which he found what was usually called the contract question.

A peculiar class of contracts is common in India, by which the planter makes advances of money to the ryot, who in return pledges himself to cultivate a particular crop on his land. In regard to many of the articles in connection with which this system prevailed, such as sugar, silk, &c., no difficulty has ever arisen; but the case in part of Bengal was otherwise where indigo was concerned.

As far back as 1830, although special legislation was not required on the subject of breaches of contract for the production of any other article of Indian agricultural produce, or, indeed, of indigo itself, except in the lower provinces of Bengal, the Indian Government deemed it necessary to make enactments for the special advantage of the indigo planter. "All persons," it was provided, " who may have received advances, and " have entered into written agreements, for the culti- " vation of indigo plant in the manner indicated in " Regulation VI. of 1823, and who, without good " and sufficient cause, shall wilfully neglect or refuse " to sow or cultivate the ground specified in such " agreement, shall be deemed guilty of misdemeanor, " and, on conviction before a magistrate or joint " magistrate, shall be liable to a sentence of imprison- " ment not exceeding one month."

The above provisions were disallowed by the Court of Directors, who considered that a law treating only one of the parties to a civil contract as a criminal if he failed to fulfil it, was manifestly unjust and oppressive.

Since that time legislation on behalf of the indigo planters has been continuously called for. They alleged that the disallowance of the penal provision of 1830 was their ruin.

Between 1854 and 1856 there was much correspondence on the subject between the Government of Bengal and its subordinate officers; but things continued in the same state, at any rate without any penal law against the ryots, until the year 1859, when the ryots refused any longer to cultivate indigo, and the Bengal indigo system came virtually to an end.

In 1860, an Act, No. XI., was passed to enforce

the fulfilment of indigo contracts during the current season. This Act contains very stringent provisions for the protection of the planter, but very lenient ones against him.

"In this special legislation," says a writer in the *Edinburgh Review*, "which was unfortunately adopted "by the Government of India for the enforcement of "indigo contracts, we have a conclusive proof of the "necessity of having a controlling authority at home "which shall be competent, vigilant, and strong."

Upon the receipt in England of the despatch forwarding this Act, Sir Charles Wood showed himself "competent, vigilant, and strong," for he lost no time in replying to the Governor-General, and on the 24th of July, 1860, he wrote :—

"The object of the Act XI. of 1860 is twofold :—
"first, to make temporary provision for enforcing by
"summary process the execution of agreements entered
"into for the cultivation of the indigo plant;—and,
"secondly, to provide for the appointment of a com-
"mission to inquire into and report on the system and
"practice of indigo planting in Bengal, and the rela-
"tions between the indigo planters and the ryots, and
"holders of land there. In regard to the first point,
"it is to be observed that the authority of the
"magistrate is to be called into action on the com-
"plaint of the planter for the enforcement of indigo
"contracts, under specified penalties, in the event
"of a failure to perform the same. The provision
"of the Act, by which a violation by a ryot of a civil
"contract, of the nature specified in the Act, is made

"the ground of a criminal prosecution by the planter,
appears to the Home Government to be open to
serious objection."

The Act however had already been brought into operation, and, being limited to the indigo season of that year, and having been passed to provide for the emergency which had suddenly arisen, was not disallowed by the Secretary of State in Council.

The system of indigo planting in Bengal, and the relation between the planter and the ryot, were notoriously of such a character as imperatively to call for inquiry. The Act of 1860 provided for the appointment of a commission for this purpose, and, in the despatch sanctioning the Act, Sir Charles Wood took the opportunity of urging the Government of India to lose no time in carrying this intention into effect.

A commission was accordingly appointed by Lord Canning, consisting of six members, two of them belonging to the Civil Service, one missionary, two native gentlemen, and the sixth Mr. Fergusson, who was specially selected as a fitting representative of the planting interest. In May, 1860, they commenced their labours, which lasted upwards of three months, and accumulated a very large and valuable mass of evidence on many points connected with the social condition of Bengal. They very properly gave prominent attention to the relations existing between the planter and the ryot, and to the elucidation of that which is in fact the pith and marrow of the whole question, viz., whether the cultivation of indigo, as carried on in Bengal, was free or forced, profitable or unprofitable, to the ryot.

That the evils complained of did not necessarily arise from the system of giving a portion of the payment in advance, at the commencement of the season, is shown by Mr. Yule, the judge of Rungpore, who thus writes on the subject:—" The great crops of " Bengal—rice, sugar, silk, fibres, oilseeds, &c.—are " advanced upon to an extent to which indigo advances " can bear no comparison. The advancers would " doubtless be glad of the aid of a summary law, but " still the ryots generally fulfil their contracts with- " out being compelled to do so, either by bands of " armed men or bribed zemindars. I fully allow " that the necessity of keeping up extensive build- " ings and a large establishment, renders a breach " of contract by the ryots more injurious to the " planter, than it is to the advancer on produce " which requires no manufacturing process to fit it " for the market; but that is no reason for changing " the law in his favour, and, if it was, it applies " to silk, sugar, lac, and other branches of trade, " as well as to indigo planting; but in all these " trades there is no general complaint that the ryots " will not fulfil their contracts; why should indigo " planting be an exception? I believe there is only " one answer to that question, and that is, in " Mr. Beaufort's words,—' Because the ryots, reason- " ' ably or unreasonably, are averse to indigo, believing " ' that there are many other crops which yield a " ' more certain as well as a better profit. I cannot

"' account for the universal dislike shown to indigo
"' by the cultivators in any other way. I cannot
"' show in figures that indigo is less profitable than
"' other crops. The ryots believe that it is so, and
"' they ought to know best. They take the advances
"' under pressure of some kind or other, and, having
"' satisfied the present necessity, endeavour to escape
"' from what they know to be a losing contract.'"

That the cultivation was unprofitable there could be little doubt, for what else had led to the "burning "indignation with which indigo planting was regarded "by the native population, and the bitter hostility "entertained amongst the ryots towards the planters "and the ruling authorities generally; what else "had led to a rising among these poor and timid "Bengalee ryots?"

The conclusion that the indigo cultivation was unprofitable to the ryot was arrived at by the commission, and was supported by an amount of evidence which was irresistible. The ryots declared that it was so, with scarcely a dissentient voice; the landholders asserted it; the missionaries affirmed it; the officers of government proved it; and the planters themselves admitted it; and they admitted more, that the ryot had been unfairly saddled with many of the expenses connected with the cultivation of indigo. The most striking and conclusive evidence of all, however, on this point, is to be found in the comparative statement in the Report of the Commission, " showing the fluctuation " or rise in the price of articles of ordinary use and " consumption, and in the remuneration for labour in "the years 1855 and 1860, in districts in which "indigo cultivation is carried on." While the price of every thing had greatly risen, in some instances to the extent of a hundred per cent., that of indigo had generally speaking been kept down to a point at which remuneration was all but impossible, and loss all but certain.

The unprofitableness of the cultivation being established, it will at once be conceded that it is not a free cultivation on the part of the ryots. The proof of this point is to be found in such abundance, in the minutes of evidence which follow the report, as to make selection the only matter of difficulty in dealing with it.

A few specimens of the statements in reference to the compulsory character of the measures adopted by the planters, and the unwillingness of the ryots to cultivate, taken from the evidence of the planter himself, will be enough, without any of the statements of the missionaries, the zemindars, or the ryots.

Mr. Sage, who had had experience of factories in Kishnaghur, Jessore, and Rungpore, when asked whether he had known of cases in which ryots were kept under restraint, first at one factory, and then at another, for the purpose of eluding the police, if their friends complained of their detention, said, "Yes, rather frequently at one time; of late years "not often; and at any time only by a very small "proportion of the planters." Again, in order to obtain a renewal of indigo contracts, "harsh treat- "ment," says Mr. Sage, "is never used until all "fair means fail;" and again, "Within your knowledge, are the ryots ever beaten by the planter?"

"Very rarely, I believe."

"Are their houses ever attacked, burnt, or thrown down?"

"Yes, I have known of such acts being done."

"Was that done to compel the ryots to take advances, or to sow in consequence of having taken advances?"

"Chiefly as a warning to others not to resist."

"Are the cattle of the ryots ever seized, with a view of inducing them to take advances?"

"I believe they are."

"Is this rare or frequent?"

"It was a general custom."

Mr. Fergusson, who represented the planters' interest in the commission, subscribed, together with Mr. Temple, a minute, in which the following statements and remarks are to be found:—

"That indigo can directly add to the wealth of the ryots, at the rates lately given, is an untenable position;" and, in his own separate minute, this gentleman says, "The recent crisis, though accelerated by an unfounded belief on the part of the ryots, that the Government was opposed to the cultivation of indigo, must have sooner or later occurred, owing to the disturbance which has taken place in the relative returns to the ryot from indigo, as compared with cereal and other cultivations; and the planters would have done well, had they paid earlier attention to the above facts, and "met the ryots with a more proportionate remuneration."

There is nothing more condemnatory of the indigo system in Bengal than the oppression practised by the native servants of the factories, and, in some instances, by the planters themselves, and the amount of violence and crime to which it has given rise.

There were cases officially reported to the Government of India, where loathsome lepers, infants, men so bedridden from age or disease as to be unable to walk, who were brought in carts and doolies, and whom it was necessary to prop up in court when their case was under trial, were charged with having received advances, under covenant, to sow and deliver Indigo plant!

Kidnapping, confining, and removing ryots from place to place, were found to have been offences of no uncommon occurrence. Mr. Sage, part of whose evidence has been quoted above, was of opinion that these cases were less common than they had been formerly. Mr. Eden, a member of the Civil Service, considered that the seizing of ryots and the confinement within factory walls had increased, as violent acts had decreased, in consequence of the establishment of numerous magisterial sub-divisions throughout Bengal. In one instance, a man had been taken from factory to factory, until he died under the treatment he received. In another, an indigo planter objected to the establishment of a deputy magistrate's court in his neighbourhood; the court was established, and no sooner was this step taken, than the discovery was made that the neighbouring factory was used as a place of illegal imprisonment for recusant or defaulting ryots.

The mode of executing contracts between the planter and the ryot also conduced to the unpopularity of the indigo cultivation; and the commissioners observed that their inquiries had placed beyond a doubt the startling fact that, in almost every concern, the contract to sow, though generally drawn up for a term of years, was renewed, or supposed to be renewed, every year, at the expense of the ryot; for, whether actually executed or not, the ryot was charged for the stamp required for the contract.

The usual mode of executing these contracts was for the ryot to put his signature or mark to a blank paper, which might be filled up or not at the discretion of the factory.

Some of the planters explained this startling fact, by alleging that the practice had been customary, and that, as the charge was a trifle, it excited no attention. Another, however, stated that the object was to keep the contract always at the full term of years for which it was originally made; and another said that the annual charge for the stamp was considered as binding the ryot. There can be little doubt that, originally, the annual renewal of a contract for a term of years was resorted to for the purpose of converting a ryot into a life cultivator for the factory; and the solution of the difficulty, if any difficulty there be, is to be found in the following pregnant sentences taken from the evidence of Mr. Cockburn, once employed as an indigo planter, now a deputy magistrate. "Many "ryots are anxious to get rid of their engagements, "and to sow no more. There were some individuals "who could clear themselves, if we would let them, "but we would not clear them, on principle, inas- "much as it would be tantamount to closing the "factory. It is my belief that many ryots would "borrow money to get free, if allowed."

In the autumn of 1860 things were indeed critical. " I assure you," said Lord Canning, " that for about " a week it caused me more anxiety than I have had " since the days of Delhi," and Lord Canning was not a man who was easily made anxious. Sir John Peter Grant, the Lieutenant-Governor of Bengal, had just returned from an excursion to the works on the Dacca railway. During his journey, which was entirely unexpected, up the river Jumoonah, numerous crowds of ryots appeared at various places, whose whole prayer was that they should not cultivate indigo. On his return, two days afterwards, from Serajgunge by the rivers Koomar and Kalligunga, which run south of the Ganges, both banks of the river for a whole day's voyage (70 or 80 miles) were lined by thousands of people, the men running by the steamer, the women sitting by the water's edge, the inhabitants of each village taking up the running in succession, and crying to him for justice, but all respectful and orderly. "The organization and capacity," said the Lieutenant-Governor, " for combined and simultaneous " action in the cause, which this remarkable demon- " stration over so large an extent of country proved, " are subjects worthy of much consideration."

"From that day," wrote Lord Canning, "I felt
"that a shot fired in anger or fear by one foolish
"planter might put every factory in Lower Bengal
"in flames."

In the spring of 1861, the report of the commission came under the consideration of the authorities at home, and the question before them was simply this:—Were criminal proceedings for breach of contract necessary? Sir Charles Wood and his Council, after a careful review of the report, were of opinion that breaches of contract ought not to entail criminal proceedings; that the relation between planters and ryots should be held to be dependent on mutual good will,—on the interest of both being fairly considered,—on proper caution being exercised in making contracts, and on integrity and forbearance. The necessity for their relations with the ryots being regulated by such considerations would not be realized by the planters, relying, as they did, on Government assistance, and the strong arm of the law being exercised in their favour against the ryot, "who," Lord Canning thought, "had been left too long in ignorance
"of the protection which he might claim against the
"proceedings of any planter who had bound him by
"unreal obligations, and who had enforced them by
"illegal means;" and the decision arrived at was ably expressed in a despatch to the Governor-General, on the 18th of April, 1861, in which, when reviewing a Bill transmitted to the Home Government, the object of which was "to provide for the punishment of
"breaches of contract, for the cultivation, production,

"gathering, provisions, manufacture, carriage, and delivery of agricultural produce," Sir Charles Wood said :—

"The question of making breaches of contract for the cultivation and delivery of agricultural produce punishable by criminal proceeding, is not one which now for the first time presents itself for consideration. It has been maturely considered, and the deliberate judgment of the Indian Law Commissioners, of the Legislative Council, of the Secretary of State in Council, of the majority of the Indigo Commissioners, of the Lieutenant-Governor of Bengal, and even, as it appears to me, of your own Government, has been recorded against any such measure. I am not prepared to give my sanction to the law which you propose, and to subject to criminal proceedings matters which have hitherto been held as coming exclusively under the jurisdiction of the civil tribunal; and I request that the Bill for the punishment of Breaches of Contract recently introduced by you into the Legislative Council may be withdrawn."

Thus has the wish strongly urged upon the Government of India by the planters, that there should be criminal punishment inflicted upon the ryots for breach of contracts, been refused and systematically discountenanced at home. The law as it existed was entirely in harmony with the view of the Indian Law Commission, under the presidency of the late Lord Macaulay, who agreed "with the great body of jurists in thinking that in general a mere breach of "contract ought not to be an offence, but only to be the subject of a civil action;" an opinion which, after being repeatedly affirmed by the ablest lawyers during twenty years, had been embodied in the Code of Law enacted only the year before this outcry for its alteration arose. Sir Charles Wood, concurring, as he did, with these views, refused to sanction an alteration of the law, and no consideration of popularity or advantage in this country, or among the planters at Calcutta, could induce him to swerve from "the great principle enunciated in his despatch," which requires that contracts between individuals shall be left in India, as in all other civilized countries, exclusively to the ordinary civil jurisdiction and process, and that "the law of India therefore shall not deviate from or violate the enlightened principles of the law of England;" and he can appeal with confidence "to the gratitude of the ryots who have been freed from the effects of a project of law opposed to the principles of civilized jurisprudence, exceptional in its aim and character, and calculated to prove an efficacious engine of injustice, hardship, and oppression."

Sir Charles Wood's desire that the Bill proposed should be withdrawn, gave rise to many complaints of his over-riding the Government of India; but this surely was a more courteous act, and less embarrassing to that Government, than if he had permitted the Bill to pass, and then refused his sanction to its enactment. Had he declined in this instance to avail himself of the controlling power vested in the Secretary of State, and allowed the Government of India to sacrifice the interests of the people to the unreasonable demands of a small interested class, he would have abdicated the real vital function of the Home Government.

Were nothing added to the foregoing remarks, it might be supposed that the law was not strong enough to give proper support to the planter when in the right. A glance at the provision of Act VIII. of 1859, and at the enactments of the penal code for the punishment of fraudulent breaches of contract and other offences committed with a view to defraud or defeat the claims of individuals, will show this not to be the case. The pressure, therefore, brought to bear upon the Government of India for special legislation has the less excuse, and the justification of the course of action adopted by Sir Charles Wood appears conclusive.

The refusal to sanction a penal contract law did not, however, definitively set at rest the indigo question. The planters knew that the ryot, more alive than formerly to the rights of his position, would not sow indigo to his own loss. The special legislation they had cried out for with so much persistency was denied to them; they feared, after the terrible exposures of the Indigo Commission, to resort to the oppression and the wrong of former times; but they were not prepared to yield without another struggle the profits hitherto reaped from the indigo crops.

Abandoning all attempts to obtain a special law for the enforcement of their contracts, they doubled the price to be paid for indigo, but, availing themselves of their position as lessees or owners of the land, they informed the ryots who occupied farms under them, that those who declined to sow indigo as heretofore would have their rents raised.

The questions involved in this "rent" dispute were, in what cases and to what extent had the zemindars of 1793, in whose place the planters now stood, the power to raise the rents of the occupying ryots.

It must be remembered that the position of the ryots in Bengal is a very peculiar one; that they have from time immemorial had some right in the soil or in its produce is universally admitted; that there exist ryots with rights of occupancy at fixed rents, and ryots with right of occupancy at rents which might be enhanced according to the rates of rent prevalent, as well as ryots who are merely tenants at will, is an undisputed fact; but the questions arising out of these rights are matters of controversy among the greatest authorities both in India and in this country.

At the time of the settlement of 1793, power had been reserved by the Government to interfere, when they deemed it necessary, for the protection of the ryot; and regulations had been at different times passed for this purpose, which were subsequently amended and embodied in the Act usually quoted as Act X. of 1859. The ryots whose rents had been fixed at the time of Lord Cornwallis's settlement, of course continued to pay the rent so fixed; and by Act X. of 1859 it was provided that twenty years' payment of the same rent should be presumptive proof that the land had been held at that rental from the time of the permanent settlement, unless the contrary be shown, or unless it be proved that such rent was fixed at some later period. In this Act it is further ruled that no ryot, having a right of occupancy at a rent which might be enhanced, shall be liable to an enhancement of rent previously paid by him, except on one of the following grounds, viz., that the rent paid by him is below the prevailing rent payable by the same class of ryots for land of a similar description, and with similar advantages, in the places adjacent; that the value of the produce, or the productive power of the land, has been increased otherwise than by the agency or at the expense of the ryot; or that the quantity of the land held by the ryot has been proved by measurement to be greater than the quantity for which rent has been previously paid by him.

In cases with right of occupancy at enhanceable rents, the rent had been generally a matter of arrangement between the zemindar and ryot, settled, in the event of a dispute, by the collector or by the village neighbours. But the British planter, who had taken the place and position of the native zemindar, with his more advanced notion of law and right, was not likely to be satisfied by such a mere rule of thumb; and the whole question, therefore, with all its complications and difficulties, was raised prominently by Mr. Hills, a planter, in a suit for the purpose of increasing the rent of one Isshur Ghose.

On the trial of this case, it was contended on the one side, by the ryot, that the rent could only be raised in proportion to the increase in the value of the produce; on the other, by the landlord, that the lessor had a right to exact as much rent as any other person would pay. The decision of the district judge was, "That it was incumbent on the plaintiff to show that "the value of the produce had increased in propor- "tion to the increase of rent asked for; and that, "if he could show that the value of the produce had "doubled, he would be entitled to recover double "the former rate of rent, and that, if it had trebled "he could treble the rent, and so on." This decision, on appeal to the higher court, was reversed by Sir Barnes Peacock and two judges sitting with him; but, on a similar action being again brought before the High Court, the case, on account of the important principle involved, was tried by the full court of fifteen judges. The whole bench, except the chief justice, pronounced against the power of the planter indefinitely to raise the rent of the ryot, and decided that the rent could only be raised in proportion to the increased value of the land, such increase not being due to the exertions of the ryot. So the matter rests for the present in Bengal.

The peculiarity of the tenure under which land is held in India, and the absence of any legal right which can be enforced in a court, were prominently brought to light during the inquiries instituted by Sir John Lawrence into the rights of the ryots under the talookdars in Oude. These inquiries gave rise to assertions that he was about to undermine and destroy the beneficial policy of Lord Canning in that province, the main feature of which was to maintain the influence and position of the talookdars.

In Oude the talookdars had acquired the possession of large districts, having holders of villages and ryots under them. On the annexation of the province by Lord Dalhousie, instructions were issued by him to set aside the talookdars altogether, so far as the settlement was concerned, merely assuring to them the payments to which they might be found entitled, and to follow the course which had been adopted in the North-West Provinces, the "leading principle" being, as was announced, "to deal with the actual " occupants of the soil, that is, with village zemindars, " or with the proprietary coparcenaries, which are " believed to exist in Oude, and not to suffer the " interposition of middlemen, as talookdars, farmers " of the revenue, and such like."

It was, as Mr. Kaye says in his history of the Sepoy war, "the policy of the time to recognize " nothing between the prince and the peasant." The settlement of Lord Dalhousie was closely followed by the mutiny of 1857, and the abrogation of the settlement followed the mutiny.

Great complaints had arisen from the village settlement; it had been found that the people did not value the rights then conferred upon them, and that in the struggle they joined their old chiefs, in spite of the oppression under which they had previously groaned. Lord Canning, therefore, determined to take advantage of the position of affairs and to reverse the former policy. Viewing the territory in the light of a conquered province, he considered himself free to do as he liked in it. He announced the confiscation of all proprietary rights; and he then issued his famous Oude proclamation, and placed the whole district under the old talookdaree system, making it a condition specified in each sunnud or grant to the talookdar, that "all holding under them should be secured in "the possession of all the subordinate rights they " formerly enjoyed."

Thus he provided, as it was thought at the time by the Government in India and at home, for the protection of the under-proprietors. The question, however, speedily arose, whether the occupying tenant generally had, or had not, a right of occupying on favourable terms. And, if Sir John Lawrence, with the firm conviction he held that the rights of these proprietors existed, and were not respected, had shrunk from the inquiry, he would not only have frustrated Lord Canning's declared intentions with regard to the humbler classes in Oude, but he would have laid himself open to the charge of sacrificing principle to expediency,—a moral cowardice totally at variance with his nature and character.

To maintain the talookdars in an influential position, possessed of administrative and judicial powers, was Lord Canning's policy, approved at home; but this policy provided also for the just rights of any small holders.

The authorities in India were not, however, of

one accord as to the extent to which those rights could be legitimately pushed, and a warm controversy arose on the subject. In the early stages of the discussion, the officers in Oude, and even the Chief Commissioner, Mr. Wingfield, thought that certain classes of the occupiers had such a right; but, in the course of the investigation, he was led to an opposite conclusion, and it was ultimately determined that an inquiry must be made as to the existence of any occupying right. This inquiry was undertaken by Mr. Davies, who was appointed Financial Commissioner in Oude.

The views of the Home Government were conveyed to the Governor-General in Sir Charles Wood's despatch of the 10th of February, 1865 :—" It would be
" a matter of deep regret to her Majesty's Government,
" if, in carrying these recent measures into execution,
" any reasonable cause of complaint was given to the
" talookdar. The just claims of subordinate holders,
" to the maintenance of which the faith of the Govern-
" ment is as much pledged as to the talookdars, must
" not be sacrificed; but I am very anxious that the
" measures ordered by your Government should not
" be pushed beyond what is indispensably requisite for
" this purpose, and that every consideration should
" be shown to the talookdars, so as not in any way to
" lower their position in the eyes of the country. I
" believe that their interests will not be injured by
" the maintenance of the rights of others, and that the
" good feeling, and, indeed, the well-being, of the
" whole community will be best promoted by the full
" recognition of the rights of all classes; but, after

"what has taken place in Oude, and the expectations
"which the talookdars have been led to entertain as
"to the effect of Lord Canning's measures, I am con-
"fident that you will see the propriety of taking especial
"care, without sacrificing the just rights of others,
"to maintain the talookdars of Oude in that posi-
"tion of consideration and dignity which Lord
"Canning's Government contemplated conferring
"upon them."

The most strenuous advocate of the rights of the talookdars has not denied that, if such proprietary rights in the soil did belong to the ryots, Lord Canning's sunnud had guaranteed their continuance; and Sir John Lawrence's inquiry, if conducted with the calm discretion and care impressed upon him by Sir Charles Wood, could only tend "to the expansion of Lord Canning's policy to its legitimate dimensions."

The result of the inquiry had not been reported when Sir Charles Wood quitted office.

CHAPTER VI.

FINANCE.

THE most pressing, and perhaps the most important matter which occupied the attention of the Government at home and in India was the state of the finances. Exhausting and distracting wars, which constantly recurred up to and during the earlier part of Lord Dalhousie's administration, had entailed on India a large military expenditure, for which the annual income had been insufficient to provide, and the deficiency had been supplied from money raised on loan.

On the termination of the last Sikh war a brighter prospect had opened on the finances of India. The last native power with which there could be any apprehension of a formidable war had been completely subdued, and everybody in India looked forward to a long period of peace and prosperity.

In each of the four years from 1849-50 to 1852-3, there was a surplus of revenue over expenditure; the price of Indian securities rose; and the interest of money fell so much that Lord Dalhousie was enabled to reduce the interest of the debt in India from five to four per cent.

But this state of financial prosperity did not last. From the years 1853-4 to 1856-7 there was a deficit every year. In 1854-5 Lord Dalhousie raised a loan of 2,750,000*l*., nominally for public works; and besides this special loan, the treasury in India was, as it had been for a long series of years, kept open for the receipt on loan of any money which persons might be disposed to pay in, on certain terms and conditions notified by public advertisement.

It is needless to point out that such a system, which relieved the Government from the necessity of providing for the annual charges out of the income of each year, was ill calculated to secure economy in the management of the public expenditure.

An enormous increase of expenditure had been the inevitable consequence of the mutiny. It had produced in the year 1857-58 an excess of charge, beyond the income, of 8,390,642*l*.; in 1858-59 a similar excess of 14,187,617*l*.; and, in the first exposition of the financial condition of India made by Sir Charles Wood in the House of Commons, on the 1st of August 1859, he stated that in the year 1859-60 the expenditure would in all probability exceed the income by no less a sum than 10,250,000*l*.

It was to be anticipated that such a prospect would be viewed with alarm by many men in and out of Parliament who were acquainted with Indian affairs; and by one distinguished orator the financial condition of India was described in the House of Commons as " a state of absolute chaos, utterly " disreputable to the past Government of India, and "presenting great difficulties to every one engaged in the attempt to restore it to a sound condition."

Without accepting that description as literally accurate, there was abundant evidence of the existence of a state of things for which it would have been idle to anticipate an adequate remedy, if the authority to whom the supreme control of Indian affairs was entrusted were deficient either in financial capacity or in firmness to carry the necessary remedial measures into effect.

To use the words of Mr. Disraeli:—"Able as has ever been the administration of India, considerable and distinguished as have been the men whom that administration has produced, and numerous as have been the great captains, the clever diplomatists, and the able administrators of large districts with whom the Government has abounded, the state of the finances has always been involved in perplexity, and India, that has produced so many great men, seems never to have produced a chancellor of the exchequer."

At that time the only prospect of improvement in the revenue was from some additions to the customs duties, and an increase of the duty on opium at Bombay, for which measures had been taken by the Government of India; but it was obvious that these would be insufficient to produce any material change in the aspect of affairs.

The expenditure on account of the army undoubtedly admitted of considerable reduction; but the increase to the debt, which was attributable to the mutiny, already entailed an additional permanent charge for interest of nearly 2,000,000*l.* per annum, which could not be reduced. With regard to the civil expenditure, it was certain that, before the administration of the country could be placed in a satisfactory condition, it would be necessary that a large increase of annual charge should be incurred on various matters connected with the administration of justice, the increase of the police, and the extension of the courts of law.

There was yet another difficulty to be encountered. The system of account in India, imperfect in itself, had become disorganized by the consequences of the mutiny, so that it was hardly practicable to obtain accurate financial returns.

The work to be taken in hand was indeed sufficiently embarrassing to excite the energies of the most ambitious financier, and was scarcely less calculated to produce some feeling of apprehension in the mind of any one who fully appreciated the magnitude of the interests at stake.

It remains to be seen how those difficulties were encountered, and how they were overcome.

It appeared to Sir Charles Wood that the first condition necessary for success was to find a fitting instrument for grappling with these questions. Fortunately a man eminently fitted for the task was at hand, and circumstances rendered it possible to send him to India.

The opportunity was not lost. A vacancy having occurred in the post of fourth ordinary member of the Governor-General's Council, which had hitherto been held by a member of the English bar, Sir Charles Wood, seeing that financial questions must, at any rate for a time, outweigh legal questions in the Council, appointed to that office Mr. James Wilson, in whom a large and comprehensive knowledge of finance and taxation was combined with habits of laborious and untiring application.

Mr. Wilson's career had indeed been remarkable, though happily not unequalled in this country. A poor apprentice to a poor shopkeeper in a small Scotch town, he had by the force of his unaided intellect and by the strength of his unwearied exertions, raised himself step by step on the ladder of fame. In a life comparatively short, he rose from an apprentice to a merchant,—in which capacity a temporary failure in the panic of 1837 only showed to more advantage the unselfish probity of his conduct; from a counting-house he passed into Parliament; and after holding office in the Board of Control, the Treasury, and the Board of Trade, and being created a Privy Councillor, he finally took his seat at the council-table of the Governor-General of India.

The leading questions of the day,—the repeal of the Corn Laws and the repeal of the Navigation Laws,— had given him ample opportunity of employing himself with his whole heart on those subjects, and he had advocated those great reforms not only by his speeches in the House of Commons and out of doors, but in the columns of the *Economist*, which he edited for many years, and in which he demonstrated, in trenchant and convincing articles, the fallacies of his opponents.

Upon these general questions of finance, taxation, currency, &c. &c., Sir Charles Wood's opinions had been formed after long and careful consideration, and confirmed by his experience whilst Chancellor of the Exchequer; and in reference to them, he had frequently communicated with Mr. Wilson. It was therefore only so far as regarded their application to India that Mr. Wilson had to learn Sir Charles Wood's views; and, before he left England, he received clear and explicit instructions as to what was to be done. It was obvious, however, that it was in India that the precise time and mode of proceeding must be determined; and upon these points Sir Charles Wood was willing to leave the Government of India unfettered by any positive directions.

On the 18th February, 1860, Mr. Wilson made his first financial statement in the council-room at Calcutta. Referring to the speech of the Secretary of State in the House of Commons in the preceding autumn, Mr. Wilson estimated the deficit for 1859-60 at 9,290,129*l.*, which was nearly a million less than the estimate of Sir Charles Wood: a favourable anticipation which was, however, not destined to be realized, as the accounts at the close of the year showed an actual deficit of 10,769,861*l.* Mr. Wilson frankly admitted that, though by the power of our arms and the courage of our civil administration, a feeling of security pervaded the country, it was "unfortunately " no State secret that an evil of the greatest magni-

"tude was corroding the very heart of our political "existence," and that it would be vain that we should boast of the restoration of order and tranquillity, if we could see no end to the financial disorder that notoriously prevailed. Looking forward to the prospect of the year 1860-61, with which he had principally to deal, he showed that, after taking credit for the reduction of a million and three-quarters in the military charges, a reduction of one million on account of compensation for losses in the mutiny, which had been included in the estimate for 1859-60, and an increase of income from the salt duty of 410,000$l.$, the expenditure of 1860-61 would still exceed the income by six and a half millions.

He stated that Lord Canning had ordered a searching investigation to be made as to the extent to which that deficit could be met by reducing expenditure, wherever practicable, but that it was apparent to the Government of India that, in addition to the work of reduction, it would be necessary to have recourse to new sources of taxation,—a great difficulty in regard to a people so simple in their habits, and consuming so few articles from which revenue can be raised, as the natives of India.

The measures selected for this purpose by the Government of India were, a revision of the customs duties, an income tax, and a licence duty; which last tax, however, was afterwards abandoned.

In dealing with the import duties which had been raised during the mutiny, the Government of India lowered them from 20 to 10 per cent. on nearly every article in the tariff: wool, hemp, hides, and jute, formerly liable to a considerable export duty, were entirely exempted, as well as tea, the experiments in its growth having shown the expediency of giving every encouragement to the attractions it held out to European capital and European settlers, and how unwise it would be to crush in its infancy an undertaking which promised so well. Saltpetre and tobacco, as exceptional articles, were subjected to an increased duty. By these changes the Government of India gave up 82,000*l*. per annum, obtained from certain customs duties, which pressed heavily on the commerce of the country, while they estimated that they would obtain, in a manner far less objectionable, 233,700*l*.

Complaints had been made by Manchester merchants at home of the unfair valuation of articles subject to customs duties, and Sir Charles Wood had promised that the matter should be set right. The leading commercial men in Calcutta were therefore called together, and, with their advice and concurrence, a revaluation was made of the articles already subject to duty, whereby an improvement of revenue was anticipated of 200,000*l*.

But all these changes, improvements though they were, were insufficient to meet the increased liabilities which pressed upon the Indian Government. Some larger measure was necessary, and the Government of India proposed an income tax of four per cent. on all incomes of 50*l*. per annum and upwards, two per cent. on incomes between 20*l*. and 50*l*., while incomes below 20*l*. were to be entirely exempted from its operation.

It was not to be expected that these taxes would be passed without some opposition. One of the objections urged against the income tax was its imputed novelty in India; but those who used this argument overlooked the fact that under the ancient Hindoo law such taxes were authorized; and it was pointed out by Sir Bartle Frere that, in the years 1834, 1835 and 1836, taxes on incomes, trades, and professions, were almost universally levied throughout British India, and that these taxes were abolished in Bengal, the North-West Provinces, and Bombay, not because they were bad in principle, but because they were so unfairly assessed, and unequally levied, that it was difficult to enforce them in their then existing shape.

The income tax, as proposed, was more, therefore, in the nature of a revival of an old, than the imposition of a new tax, and, with the exemptions and alterations that were adopted subsequently to its introduction, it was not calculated to press with great severity on any class of the natives.

The smaller proprietors would escape payment altogether, while the tax was intended to bring under assessment the richer landholders and merchants who hitherto had contributed absolutely nothing to the public burthens. It was alleged that such a tax, as regarded the landholders, was a breach of the perpetual settlement; but even influential natives of India admitted the fallacy of that objection; and one of them, the Maharajah of Burdwan, repudiated the allegation in the following words:—" I cannot," he said, "find anything in the terms of the settlement " to convince me that the zemindaries of India have " for ever been exempted from contributing to assist " the Government, when they incur unavoidable " expenses in preserving property, life, the honour " and all that is dear to them, of those very " zemindars."

No opposition to the tax, however, occcasioned so much anxiety as that of the Governor of Madras, Sir Charles Trevelyan, who protested against its imposition on the people of that presidency. Had such a protest come to the Governor-General as a confidential communication, it would have been a fitting and proper proceeding, and the opinion of the Governor of Madras was entitled to the greatest consideration; but Sir Charles Trevelyan not only wrote a minute on the subject, but published it, warning the Government that the south of India had twice come to the aid of the Government in the north in their hour of need; and he added, " One " hundred years elapsed between those two occasions; " but it is impossible to say how soon a third may " arise, and it would be impolitic to unite the south " with the north of India in a common cause " against us."

It was a serious matter that the Governor of Madras should be opposed to the imposition of a tax deemed absolutely necessary by the Government of India. The publication of his minute condemning the tax was not only a breach of public duty, but was calculated to produce a most prejudicial effect on the native mind, and to cause much embarrassment to the Government of India in a moment of great difficulty, when they were entitled to expect the assistance of all the public servants. The Secretary of State was so deeply impressed with the necessity of giving all the support in his power to the Government of India at such a crisis, that he immediately recalled Sir Charles Trevelyan.

That duty was one of the most painful that could well be imposed on Sir Charles Wood; for Sir Charles Trevelyan was his personal friend, and had served for many years under him in the Treasury at home, and, while continuing the useful measures instituted by Lord Harris, and supplementing these with others of his own devising, he had conducted the government of Madras in a manner which had done much to heal the wounds that had previously existed among its population, and to bring that population to regard the English rule with favourable feelings. Indeed, in another despatch, written on the same day as the one recalling him, Sir Charles Wood, in thanking him for his valuable services, took occasion to remark, that "no servant of the Crown had more earnestly "endeavoured to carry out the great principles of "Government which were promulgated to the pro-"vinces and people of India in her Majesty's pro-"clamation."

Some demonstrations took place in other parts of India against the imposition of the tax, but the Act was passed. Happily, the judgment, ability, and conciliatory spirit in which the tax was levied by the English officials overcame many of the objections which had been felt to it, and secured the co-operation and good will of the more respectable classes of the native community.

The reduction of the annual expenditure was, if possible, a subject of greater importance and difficulty than the increase of taxation.

In 1856-57 the total expenditure of India, including guaranteed interest on railway capital, amounted to 33,852,234*l.*; in 1859-60 the expenditure had risen to no less than 50,475,683*l*. To reduce this enormous annual charge within moderate dimensions needed all the anxious attention of Sir Charles Wood; but, in effecting that great object, he could hardly have desired heartier aid than he received from Lord Canning, nor could he have found an abler or more indefatigable assistant than Mr. Wilson; and it was in India that the practical reductions that were required must be made.

It was obvious that little in the way of reduction was to be expected in the civil administration; as it was conducted already on principles of economy, " at a smaller cost than that of any country in the " world."

With regard to the military expenditure, the imperative necessity of effecting every practicable reduction had been pressed on the Government of India by Lord Stanley, as Secretary of State; and in April, 1859, the Governor-General called on Colonel (now Major-General) Jameson, the auditor-general at

Bombay, for his opinion as to the best mode of effecting those reductions.

Having been put in possession of that officer's opinions on the subject, the Government of India appointed a military finance commission, consisting of Colonel Jameson as president, and Colonels Burn and Balfour as members.

The commission first assembled on the 18th of July, 1859, and reported from time to time as to the reductions that could be effected. In January, 1860, they submitted a report on the existing system of account and audit, and made propositions for effecting important reforms therein, and they pointed out the necessity that existed for the preparation of an annual budget of military expenditure. The propositions contained in that report were important, not only in regard to the more immediate object for which the commission had been appointed, but as also indicating other changes in the Indian system of estimate, account, and audit, which were subsequently, as will be hereafter seen, entered upon and carried out, greatly to the benefit of the Indian Government.

In April, 1860, Colonel Burn was compelled by ill-health to leave India, and in June following the commission was deprived of the valuable services of its president, Colonel Jameson. Lieutenant-Colonel Simson and Mr. Richard Temple were afterwards added to the commission, and the Government of India bore ample testimony to the important services which that commission rendered, as well as to the benefits which resulted from the labours of Colonel Balfour, who was appointed chief of the Military Finance Department, and who ably and energetically carried out the work of reduction and reform which had been suggested.

In dealing with the military charges, Mr. Wilson saw clearly how large reductions could be made, not indeed in the pay and emoluments of either officers or men, but in the numerical strength of the army, by a better distribution of the forces, by control over the commissariat and other expenditure, and, to use his own words, " by reducing our army finance to order."

In applying himself to that work, Mr. Wilson introduced the system of preparing annually a budget of income and expenditure, in order to bring before the Supreme Government, for sanction at the commencement of each year, carefully devised estimates of expenditure in every department, thereby guarding against irregular and unauthorized outlays for which no adequate provision had been made in the ways and means of the year. At the same time, within the limits sanctioned by the Government of India, a greater latitude than had before been given, was allowed to the subordinate Governments of Madras and Bombay.

In maturing the scheme which the Government of India had determined on introducing, Mr. Wilson laboured unremittingly, setting at nought the advice of his physicians, despising the warnings of a fatal and insidious disease, and perhaps not admitting to himself how valuable the continuance of his health and working powers had become to India.

It was in August that he was first attacked by

sickness, but he nevertheless continued to discharge without intermission his public duties.

Work at night, the habitual custom of an English politician, is notoriously unhealthy, if not fatal, in India. Although fully aware of this danger, night after night, when others found repose from the weariness which follows hard work in a Calcutta climate, Mr. Wilson would rise and set to work, till absolute exhaustion compelled him once more to seek the rest which he was unable to obtain.

A trip to sea was talked of—that wonderful panacea for all the enervating diseases of India; but it was too late. A few days sufficed to render his illness fatal. Lord Canning visited the sick man on his death-bed, and was deeply touched by the tone in which he spoke of public matters. Not a word of self, or of his name or share in public affairs, escaped his lips. He expressed his hopefulness of the success of the great work in which he had been engaged, and calmly died, adding another name to that long list of heroes, who, at the desk as well as in the more exciting scenes of battle, have, without a complaint or murmur, laid down their lives in India in their country's service.

"Nothing can replace," wrote one of his fellow-councillors, "the ripe experience and practical sagacity which tempered the unfailing energy of the colleague we have lost," and Sir Charles Wood deeply felt the loss of so able a coadjutor.

It was obviously advisable that there should be no delay in appointing a successor, and the choice fell on Mr. Laing, Secretary to the Treasury in Lord

Palmerston's Government, who was appointed member of Council in Mr. Wilson's place.

On Mr. Laing's acceptance of this appointment, Sir Charles Wood took occasion to urge with, if possible, increased force, the absolute necessity of early and vigorous exertions on the part of the Government of India in the reduction of expenditure, wherever it could be effected without neglecting the indispensable requirements of the public service.

"I cannot," he said, "allow myself to contem-
" plate any further increase in the taxation of India,
" and I can hardly think that any attempt at imposing
" additional burthens would not be attended by in-
" creased difficulty and cost of collection, beyond any
" possible advantage of increased receipts, indepen-
" dently of the obvious evil of the unpopularity of any
" such measure."

The Government of India applied itself with unflinching energy to the work of reduction, and, as early as February, 1861, Sir Charles Wood was enabled to anticipate the favourable results of his instructions and of their exertions, and, both in his despatches to the Governor-General in Council and by his speeches in Parliament, he indicated the measures by which he considered that in the year 1861-62 the expenditure could be brought within the income. He showed that the reductions ordered by the Government of India were expected to amount in the year 1860-61 to 2,500,000*l*., which, with those of the previous year would make an estimated saving in military expenditure alone, of 6,000,000*l*. ; and that, if the reductions for 1861-62 were equal to those of 1860-61, and the produce of the new taxes came up to the estimate, the deficit would be extinguished, and the expenditure and income of 1861-62 would be balanced. The Government of India at that time looked upon Sir Charles Wood's financial statement as too sanguine, and there were many at home who shared the gloomy anticipations of that Government, but it was subsequently demonstrated, when the accounts were made up, that his views were almost literally correct, the deficit of 1861-62 being only 50,628*l*.

Although, however, the Government of India were, in February, 1861, unable to foresee the probable accomplishment at so early a period of the equalization of income and expenditure, too much praise cannot be given to them for their ready co-operation in the measures by which that great object was attained; and on no individual should greater praise be bestowed than on Sir George Clerk, for his unceasing and successful efforts in reducing the military expenditure in Bombay.

In June, 1862, Mr. Laing's health, unsuited for official life in an Indian climate, compelled him to return to England.

In looking for a successor, Sir Charles Wood's attention was not unnaturally turned to Sir Charles Trevelyan, whose fitness for employment in India could hardly be overlooked. He had commenced his career as a Bengal civilian. For twenty years he had been Secretary to the Treasury at home; but here, with a constant strain on his energies, he had not forgotten his old associations and interests in India, and the letters of "Indophilus" which appeared from time to time had not only attracted the attention but had taken a great hold of the minds of those at home to whom India was not, as it is to many, a *terra incognita*. He had shown himself an excellent Indian administrator during his short rule at Madras. It is true that he had committed one great indiscretion, but he had paid a severe penalty in being recalled from so honourable a position. His recall had been to Sir Charles Wood a very painful, though necessary duty, and he gladly welcomed the opportunity of again rendering the services of so able an administrator available for the public good.

It was doubted, however, whether, after having been governor of a presidency, Sir Charles Trevelyan would again undertake a subordinate appointment with less responsible duties. Many men of smaller minds would have shrunk from the acceptance of such an appointment, but the offer generously made was met by him in a similar spirit; and in the commencement of 1863 Sir Charles Trevelyan set out on his third journey to India, as member of the Governor-General's Council.

The small excess of expenditure over income, amounting to 50,628*l.* in the year 1861-62, was followed in 1862-63 by a surplus of income over expenditure of no less an amount than 1,827,346*l.*; but this was an exceptional occurrence, and was mainly due to an unprecedented receipt from opium, the produce of which in that year was 8,055,476*l.*, or 1,696,207*l.* more than had been realized on the same account in 1861-62. In the year 1863-64, the income exceeded the expenditure by only 78,347*l*., and here again the change from the previous year nearly corresponds with the falling off in the net proceeds of the opium revenue: the receipt from that source of income in 1863-64 having been less by 1,223,477*l*. than the amount obtained in 1862-63, while the cost and charges of the drug were 450,215*l*. more than in the former year.

In 1864-65, the expenditure again exceeded the income by 193,521*l*., and this is the last year for which the accounts have been received. For the year 1865-66, reference can be made to estimates only; these once more show an excess of income over expenditure of 20,585*l*.

In order to see how far the change from an excess of expenditure over income in 1859-60 of 10,769,861*l*. to an excess of only 50,628*l*. in 1861-62, and the subsequent continuance of a state of comparative equilibrium of income and expenditure, was attributable to increases of revenue or reduction of charge, it is necessary to refer shortly to the total amount realized and expended in each year, and to the principal heads under which changes occurred. The total revenues and receipts in India amounted in

		£
1858-59 to	....	36,060,788
1859-60 ,,	....	39,705,822
1860-61 ,,	....	42,903,234
1861-62 ,,	....	43,829,472
1862-63 ,,	....	45,143,752
1863-64 ,,	....	44,613,032
1864-65 ,,	....	45,652,897
1865-66 ,, (estimated)	.....	47,041,540

being an increase of income for 1865-66, as compared with 1858-59, of 10,980,752*l.*

Of that increase nearly two millions were derived from the land revenue, which, under an improved system of assessment, shows a continuous advance.

About four and a half millions were obtained from new or increased taxes, nearly two and a half millions from opium, the remaining two millions consisting of improved receipts from existing taxes consequent on the general prosperity of the country.

The charges in India and England during the same period were as follows:—

	£
1858-59	50,248,405
1859-60	50,475,683
1860-61	46,924,619
1861-62	43,880,100
1862-63	43,316,407
1863-64	44,534,685
1864-65	45,846,418
1865-66 (estimated)	47,020,955

The total charges were therefore lowest in the year 1862-63, when the effect of the stringent measures of reduction which were adopted to bring the expenditure within the income was fully realized, and the reductions were almost wholly in the military charges. Those reductions, indeed, greatly exceeded the sum of seven millions, the net reduction on the total charge, there having been considerable increases in some of the civil departments.

The period for which the income tax had been imposed, terminated in August, 1865, and, when the budget of 1865-6 was under the consideration of the

Government of India, it was decided that there was not sufficient ground for its reimposition. Whatever opinion may be entertained as to the expediency of that decision, it must be admitted that keeping faith to the very letter in matters of finance, even where a doubt exists as to the engagements, may be worth more in India than an overflowing treasury.

The budget of 1865-6 was, nevertheless, open in other respects to serious objections. In order to make good a part of the loss caused by the cessation of the income tax, Sir Charles Trevelyan proposed to collect export duties on several articles of Indian produce, to raise in England a loan of 1,200,000*l*., and to include the sum so raised as a part of the revenue of the year, thus producing an appearance of a surplus when a deficit was really to be anticipated.

It was not by such measures as these that the finances of India had been placed on the footing that they then occupied. After revising the budget and acquiescing in the repeal of the income tax, Sir Charles Wood condemned the loan, and disallowed the proposed export duties. He was thus compelled, with no small regret, to admit a prospective deficit for the year 1865-6 of 375,000*l*.

After the publication of his budget, failing health compelled Sir Charles Trevelyan to return to England, and Sir Charles Wood was able to secure the services of Mr. Massey as the financial member of the Governor-General's Council. Mr. Massey had already filled with considerable credit the post of Under-Secretary to the Home Office, and was, at the time of his appointment to India, the Chairman of Ways and Means in the House of Commons.

The budget of the Government of India for 1866-67, the first after Mr. Massey's appointment, had not been received in England at the time of Sir Charles Wood's retirement from office, and therefore did not come under his review. It may be observed, however, that there was nothing in that budget to raise any doubt as to the wisdom of the selection of Mr. Massey for carrying on the work which had been for years in progress under Sir Charles Wood's directions.

Sir Charles Wood's financial administration of India may be briefly summarized as follows :—

On taking office he had to face an expenditure of 50,475,000*l*., with an income of 39,705,000*l*. ; to provide by loan for the deficiency of income, with the credit of Indian securities seriously impaired ; and, insufficient as the means of India were to meet the current expenditure on public works, to raise funds for an increased outlay on that account.

He resigned office with the annual income adequate to the expenditure, with Indian credit thoroughly re-established, and this notwithstanding a considerable increase in the amount expended on public works.

It is in consequence of that success that we are now able to look upon India, not in the light of a burden on the British taxpayer, or a borrower on the British Stock Exchange, but as a solvent state, willing and able to assist us with valuable commodities, and to pay for all her own internal improvements.

In 1856-57, the year before the mutiny, her imports amounted to 28,608,284*l.*, and her exports to 26,591,877*l.*, while in 1864-5, the last year for which reliable returns have been received, the imports amounted to 48,702,260*l.*, and the exports to 66,537,886*l.*, showing on the whole an increase of trade of upwards of 98 per cent. in eight years.

" The future resources of India," says the Quarterly reviewer, " are quite incalculable. We have already " seen her replacing with her produce the hemp and " linseed of Russia, and the cotton of America ; she is " rapidly preparing to substitute her tea for that of " China. Should England ever be cut off from her " usual sources of supply of sugar, coffee, silk, wool, " or iron, in a few years India could make good the " deficit. Even now India supplies a fair proportion " of these articles, and Indian labour produces a large " proportion of the supply from our colonies. So " long as India and England are allied, England is " independent of the rest of the world."

It may be safely asserted, therefore, that the financial measures of Sir Charles Wood's administration have been numerous and successful, beyond all reasonable expectation, and that his comprehensive knowledge and great capacity in dealing with all matters relating to finance have been of the greatest value in retrieving the Indian exchequer from the disastrous state into which it had fallen.

It was not however solely to the possession of those qualities, but also to his knowledge of men, and judgment in his choice of them, that much of his success is to be attributed. Those whom he selected as his instruments in India have been already pointed out; and in the India Office he found that he could place implicit reliance, not only on the members of his finance committee, but also on his financial secretary, Mr. Seccombe, whose great knowledge of his business, perfect accuracy, and unflinching application to his work, obtained for him the entire confidence of Sir Charles Wood.

A question far less interesting to the public, but one which required much thought and labour, was the improvement of the Indian system of account; and, although the time has not yet arrived when the full extent of the benefits of the measures adopted by him can be appreciated, sufficient experience has been obtained to give reason for hoping that a foundation has been laid for a thoroughly good system of estimate, account, and audit, which only needs time to be fully developed.

The Indian accounts had been unnecessarily complicated and diffuse, and in the year following the mutiny had fallen hopelessly into arrear. There were not, it was thought, men in India qualified for the work of revising the mode of keeping the accounts, so as to make them harmonize with the new forms of estimate; and, therefore, at the instance of Sir Charles Trevelyan, two commissioners were sent from England, for the purpose of completing a system very similar in detail to that which is now adopted by all the principal offices of Government in this country.

These commissioners, Mr. Foster, Assistant Paymaster-General, and Mr. Whiffin, an Assistant Accountant-General at the War Office, have concluded their labours and returned to England; and there is reason to hope that it will be found that the changes that have been made, will go far towards remedying the serious evils which had been so long acknowledged and deplored.

CHAPTER VII.

CURRENCY.

THE improvement of the currency of India, by the introduction of a system of paper money better calculated than the notes of the Banks of Bengal, Madras, and Bombay to obtain general circulation, was a question intimately connected with Indian finance.

On this subject Sir Charles Wood was entitled to speak with great authority, from the knowledge which he had obtained as chairman of the parliamentary committee on the Bank Acts in 1841, from the part which he had taken in the discussions on the Bank of England Charter Act in 1844, and from the experience he acquired while Chancellor of the Exchequer in the monetary crisis of 1847.

Before describing the paper currency introduced under Sir Charles Wood's instructions, it will be well to glance briefly at the monetary system previously existing in India.

The rupee of 180 troy grains weight, containing 165 grains of pure silver, and of the value of about two shillings, constitutes, with the exception of copper, nearly the whole circulating medium of India, and it was, and still continues to be, the measure of value in

British India. The mohur, a gold coin identical in weight and fineness with the rupee, was coined to a small extent at the Government mints, but was not received at Government treasuries in payment of revenue since 1852, and circulated as coin to a very small extent.

There was also a limited circulation of bank-notes, confined almost exclusively to the presidency cities. They were issued by the Banks of Bengal, Madras, and Bombay, in each of which the Government was a shareholder, and was directly represented on the board of management by public officers, appointed under the designation of Government directors.

The authorized circulation of those banks was as follows :—

	£
Bank of Bengal, 2 crores of rupees, or	2,000,000
Bank of Madras, 1 ,, ,,	1,000,000
Bank of Bombay, 2 ,, ,,	2,000,000

The actual circulation of the Bank of Bengal was somewhat within that limit; that of the Bank of Bombay was usually under 1,000,000*l.*; while that of the Bank of Madras rarely amounted to 200,000*l.*

Throughout the vast territories of the Indian empire, therefore, silver coin formed practically the only means of discharging debts or defraying expenditure; and, although silver coin was inconveniently bulky for transmission to great distances, it was not supplemented by any popular gold coin, or any acceptable form of paper money.

The Government was compelled, in consequence of the imperfect means of communication, to maintain treasuries, with large amounts of cash, in charge of Government officers, for carrying on the receipts and payments of the State. It is easy to understand that, in the absence of a paper or gold currency, the constant transmission of large sums in silver coin between the Government treasuries was a work of great labour, risk, and expense; but it would be difficult to convey to the mind of a person unacquainted with India, the extent to which the army of the East India Company had for years been employed in detachments as treasure escorts.

The question of introducing a more extended paper currency into India had frequently been discussed, and Sir Charles Wood thought that the time had arrived when such a measure might be adopted with great advantage. It was his wish to establish a paper circulation, issued directly by Government, and conducted on the principle which had been laid down and enforced in the Bank Act of 1844, *i.e.*, that a certain fixed amount of notes, corresponding as nearly as could be ascertained to the minimum ordinary circulation of the country, should be issued against an equal sum to be held in Government securities, and that notes in excess of that amount should be issued only against bullion or coin to be held in the currency department.

Before Mr. Wilson went to India, the whole subject of currency was fully discussed with him by Sir Charles Wood, and a general plan was devised, which was afterwards developed in an able minute by Mr. Wilson, written soon after his arrival in India.

In that paper Mr. Wilson discussed with his characteristic clearness the advantages to be obtained from the general use of bank-notes, and he showed that, in order to secure the confidence of the people, it was necessary that the notes should be issued under the direct authority and management of the Government.

The main features of the plan were:—

1st. The withdrawal of the privileges of issue hitherto enjoyed by the three presidency banks.

2nd. The issue of notes by the Government at the three cities of Calcutta, Madras, and Bombay, and in circles at various places in the interior of the country, the notes issued in any circle being payable only in that circle and at the presidency cities.

3rd. That coin or bullion, to the extent of one-third of the notes issued, should always be kept in the currency departments, and Government securities held for the remainder.

With the exception of the last provision, Mr. Wilson's plan was in accordance with the arrangements of the issue department of the Bank of England; but the exception was important, and was a departure from Sir Charles Wood's instructions.

While this scheme was under discussion, Mr. Wilson died, and Mr. Laing, who succeeded him, was desired by Sir Charles Wood to endeavour to amend the proposed plan in this respect, and to adhere strictly to the principles enforced in the Act of 1844.

The amendment was carried into effect by the Government of India, but they deviated from the intentions of Sir Charles Wood in another respect, by making the banks in the presidency cities the agents for the issue and exchange of notes.

Under the system which was adopted, the notes were to be of the denominations of 10, 20, 50, 100, 500, and 1,000 rupees. The expediency of issuing a five-rupee note was duly considered and provided for in the Bill introduced into the Legislative Council of India, Sir Charles Wood and Mr. Wilson being in its favour; but the special committee of the Legislative Council altered the Bill, so as to exclude notes of five rupees, a change in regard to which Sir Charles Wood at once expressed his disapproval.

Ten circles have been established up to the present time:—Calcutta, with Allahabad, Lahore, and Nagpore as branches; Madras, with Calicut, Trichinopoly, and Vizagapatam as branches; Bombay, with a branch at Kurrachee.

The amount of notes to be issued on Government securities was not to exceed four crores of rupees, or 4,000,000*l*., an amount somewhat in excess of the former circulation of the three presidency banks, which, as has been seen, seldom reached 3,200,000*l*.

The circulation of the new notes has increased, and on the 31st of October last had reached the sum of 10,160,959*l*.

Although, when compared with the notes issued by the three presidency banks, the circulation of Government notes shows a great augmentation, the issue in the circles has not, as yet, reached the amount which had been expected. Comparatively few notes have been taken out for local use, but further experience of their convenience will, it is to be anticipated, increase their popularity in the country; and there can be no doubt but that the issue of a note of a smaller denomination than ten rupees, according to Sir Charles Wood's intentions, would lead to that result.

In carrying the currency scheme into effect, the claims of the three presidency banks to some compensation for the withdrawal of the privilege of issuing notes were not overlooked. An arrangement was made, whereby not only were those claims satisfied, but the banks were made the bankers of the Government at the presidency cities and at certain places in the interior, and they have been subsequently entrusted with the detailed management of the Government debt. In pursuance of that arrangement, the balances in the Government treasuries at the places referred to were made over to the banks, and a minimum balance was fixed, which the Government was to keep in their hands.

These arrangements necessitated the grant of new charters to the three banks. In the terms of those charters the Government of India allowed a provision to be inserted which involved a departure from Sir Charles Wood's intentions, as it authorized the banks, in regard to their agency department, to draw bills payable out of India, and to purchase bills for the purpose of providing funds to meet those drafts, a form of dealing in exchanges whereby they might incur risks inconsistent with the prudent management imperatively required on the part of any bank connected with the Government, and in whose hands the Government money was kept.

It was difficult, however, for Sir Charles Wood to disallow that provision, as it could only be done by refusing his assent to the Act constituting the charter. As the agreement with the banks was to be in force for only five years, he entrusted the rectification of that error to the Government of India. It was, however, a work of considerable difficulty, and was not accomplished until Sir Charles Trevelyan had succeeded Mr. Laing as financial member of the Governor-General's Council, when, after much correspondence with the bank, an arrangement was made by which that objectionable part of the agreement was terminated.

The Act authorizing the issue of a Government paper currency contained one other provision which gave rise to some anxiety during a time of pressure for coin at Bombay. Under section ix. of that Act, notes were to be issued in exchange for bullion or coin, the currency commissioner being entitled to require such bullion or coin to be melted and assayed. The notes were issued as soon as the bullion was assayed, and there was no provision that any time must be allowed for coining the bullion into rupees. In regard to bullion taken direct to the mint for coinage, provision was made for an interval between the deposit of the bullion and the delivery of the coin; but, under this section of the Currency Act, a person taking bullion to the currency department received notes at once, and, as the currency department was bound to give coin for notes immediately, if demanded, it followed that, by this double action, the Government might be called upon to deliver at once an amount of coin which they had not had the time or opportunity of providing.

But, although some risk of inconvenience was incurred, actual embarrassment was avoided, and, under Sir Charles Wood's directions, the rules for granting notes in exchange for bullion have been so modified as to preclude the occurrence of any similar risk in future.

The time that has elapsed since the introduction of the Government paper currency is not sufficient to show what will be its real value in the monetary system of India, when the use of the notes shall be more fully understood and appreciated, and a lower denomination of note brought into use. Enough, however, has been stated to show that, whereas, on Sir Charles Wood's acceptance of the office of Secretary of State for India, that country was practically without any useful paper money, he introduced a paper currency based on sound principles; and, when he quitted office, the system was so far in operation as to leave it a comparatively easy task to carry it into effect, to whatever extent the wants of India may require.

The question of introducing gold coins more largely into the currency of India had also been considered by Sir Charles Wood, and discussed by him with Mr. Wilson; and, as the latter had placed on record the result of their deliberations when dealing with the paper currency in his minute dated the 25th of December, 1859, so, in another minute bearing the same date, he discussed the subject of the introduction of a gold currency into India. He admitted that, if the system of currency were to be commenced de novo, there would be a manifest convenience in having a gold coin as the standard, and silver tokens as subordinate coins. But, as all contracts in India were made in silver, he was of opinion that the contract between debtor and creditor must be strictly maintained. Nor did he consider that any important advantage would attend the use of gold, if it were otherwise practicable. He remarked that the expense of removing coin was in a small degree only determined by its weight and bulk, to a much greater extent by the necessity of protecting it, and that it was doubtful whether there would not be somewhat more danger of robbery from local treasuries containing gold, than if they contained silver. He concluded his minute by expressing his opinion that a well-regulated paper currency was more suited to the wants of India than a currency consisting mainly of gold.

The question of a gold currency was not again raised until the year 1864, when the Bengal, Madras, and Bombay Chambers of Commerce represented to the Government of India that it would be expedient to introduce gold as an auxiliary currency, the Bombay Chamber of Commerce adding that India was not yet prepared for a paper currency.

The subject was freely discussed by the members of the Government of India, and in July, 1864, in forwarding a minute by Sir Charles Trevelyan, that Government expressed its concurrence in his proposition that sovereigns and half-sovereigns, of the British and Australian standard, coined at any properly authorized royal mint in England, Australia, or India, should be made legal tender throughout the British dominions in India, at the rate of one sovereign for ten rupees.

In replying to the Government of India, Sir Charles Wood observed that there could not be any doubt of the advantage to India, England, and Australia, if the gold sovereign could be made the basis of their common currency. He objected, however, to the proposal of that Government, which would have the effect of establishing a double standard of gold and silver. He showed that, at the existing price of silver, a sovereign was worth intrinsically more than ten rupees, and that an enactment making the sovereign a legal tender for less than it was worth, would be practically inoperative. He further stated that, at the present relative value of gold and silver, the question whether the sovereign would circulate at ten rupees could only be determined by experience; and, in order to give every facility for trying the experiment, he requested the Government of India to notify by proclamation that, until further notice, sovereigns and half-sovereigns of the British and Australian standard, coined at any properly authorized mint in England or Australia, and of current weight, would be received in all the treasuries of India for the same sum as ten and five silver rupees respectively, and would, unless objected to, be paid out again at the same rate.

Since 1864 no change has been made in regard

to the receipt of sovereigns in India, and, as in most other questions relating to currency, various opinions have been expressed as to the necessity for, and the best mode of, introducing gold, and especially the sovereign, more generally into use.

In the year just closed the Government of India, having received a memorial from the Bengal Chamber of Commerce, praying for an inquiry as to the expediency of introducing gold into the monetary system of India, appointed a commission " to inquire into " the operation of the Paper Currency Act, upon any " improved arrangements, including the introduction " of notes for five rupees, by which it could be rendered " more effective; and upon any extension of the mone- " tary system, which the increasing commerce and " prosperity of the country may seem to require;" that inquiry being considered by the Government of India a necessary preliminary to any consideration of the question of taking further measures for the introduction of gold.

The report of that committee has not yet been received in England.

CHAPTER VIII.

LAND REVENUE.

A VERY large portion of the income of India is derived immediately from the land. Next in order come salt and opium, customs and stamps; but, even when taken together, they do not usually give so large a return as is obtained under the heading of Land ; indeed, before the mutiny, more than half the revenues of India were derived from that source; and in the year 1865-66 it was estimated at 20,066,200*l*., in a total income of 47,041,540*l*.

A prominent event in the revenue administration of India, during the period now under review, is the publication by Lord Canning, in October, 1861, of a resolution "regarding the sale of waste lands in fee "simple, and the redemption of existing land revenue."

The proposals of the Government of India were to the effect that all unoccupied waste lands throughout British India should be sold to any buyers, at a fixed price of five shillings per acre for uncleared, and ten shillings per acre for cleared, lands. For thirty days after an intending purchaser had put in his application, any one claiming the property applied for might assert his right to it; if, however, that period of thirty days elapsed without any claim being advanced, the property was to be allotted to the applicant, whose absolute possession was not hereafter to be disturbed, even if a right of property in the land so allotted should be established.

Compensation might be awarded to any one proving a title to the land within a year of the sale; but the original possessor was not allowed to have any claim for the restoration of his land.

Most delusive ideas were entertained by many as to the advantages likely to ensue from this resolution of the Government of India. Energetic capitalists were supposed to be only waiting for the opportunities thus presented to them, to flock to the jungles of India, and convert the howling wilderness into a smiling cotton-field. The Government of India itself was not entirely free from these utopian anticipations; it was confidently hoped "that harmony of interests between permanent European settlers and the half-civilized tribes by whom most of the waste districts and the country adjoining them are thinly peopled, will conduce to the material and moral improvement of large classes of the Queen's Indian subjects, which for any such purposes have long been felt by the Government to be almost out of the reach of its ordinary agencies." Sir Charles Wood, on the contrary, perceived that European settlers and wild tribes, in tracts of country far removed from the protection of the law, were little likely to form themselves into a peaceful and harmonious community, bound together by the mutual interests of trade and commerce. The intrusion of European settlers amongst warlike and predatory clans, passionately attached to their ancestral lands, would lead to differences and quarrels ending in bloodshed, and the ultimate extermination of the weaker body. The Government of India was therefore cautioned to exercise the greatest care " in allowing grants of land in outlying districts, where the arrangements for the protection of life and property were still imperfectly organized."

The quantity of really unoccupied land in India, except in wild and remote districts, has been generally very much exaggerated. A traveller passing up the country saw extensive jungles and apparent wastes, and not unnaturally inferred that these tracts were unoccupied and unclaimed by any one. This was, however, far from being the case. " The assumption " that these lands," wrote Lord Canning, " were unen- " cumbered with private rights and tenures, was erro- " neous, and the publication of such statements was " extremely mischievous." Nearly the whole of them belonged to some proprietor or another,—the neighbouring zemindar in Bengal, or the inhabitants of an adjacent village, to whom they afforded pasture for their cattle; and the sale of such land would be as much an act of confiscation, as it would be if an unenclosed sheepwalk in Sussex was seized on, and sold by the order of the magistrates at quarter-sessions. It was pointed out to the Indian Government that the mode proposed by them for securing to the grantees the possession of their land, without regard to the rights of original claimants, was not only entirely inconsistent with equity, but also with the provisions of the law, which could only be altered, if it were considered necessary to do so, by legal enactment.

The land which was really available for sale by Government consisted nearly altogether of wild districts in remote parts of India, in Assam, Oude, or the Central Provinces; and as to such lands Sir Charles Wood approved of the proposed resolutions, with only two exceptions. In the first place, he insisted that a rough survey of the land, sufficient to ascertain the identity and quantity of the lots, should be made previously to, instead of after, the sale of the land. Such a survey would appear to be a necessary preliminary to a sale being effected or a purchase made, as without it a purchaser would really be in ignorance of what property he had bought; and it entailed no expensive European agency. "Hundreds " of native surveyors," said the Chief Commissioner of Oude, "trained in Government schools, and therefore " capable of performing the work, are available." Sir Charles Wood further desired that on all occasions the land to be sold should be put up to auction, as is the invariable practice in Ceylon, instead of being sold at a price fixed irrespective of the value of the soil, its situation, capacities for irrigation, and contiguity to roads.

Abundant evidence has already been forthcoming that the provision requiring all waste lands to be put up to auction has in many cases secured large sums for the land purchased, and has effectually prevented land-jobbing on the part of speculators. In some cases as much as 8*l*. per acre has been realized by the Government, instead of the small fixed sum at which it was proposed that they should be sold.

Rules have been since drawn up by the several local governments in accordance with Sir Charles Wood's directions, and a tribunal has been established for the adjudication of all claims to lands proposed to be sold.

By the same resolution of October, 1861, Lord Canning authorized the redemption of the land-tax, whether permanently or temporarily settled, to the extent of one-tenth of the aggregate amount of the assessment in each district.

Sir Charles Wood objected to this resolution. There was no source of income so little unpopular as the land revenue, and he disliked the sacrifice of so large a portion of that safe and secure income which was always to be depended on. It had been disapproved of by the great majority of the ablest officers in India. It was improbable that many persons would avail themselves of the power of redemption; indeed, when the experiment had been tried in the North-West Provinces and Oude, during six months after the publication of the Government resolutions not a single landowner had applied for a redemption of his land-tax. Apart from this resolution, it was already in the power of any landholder in Bengal practically to redeem his land-tax, by placing in the hands of the Collector an amount of public securities the interest of which was equal to the rent of his estate; but for thirty years hardly anybody had availed himself of this power.

Sir John Lawrence also deprecated a policy, the effect of which he knew, if fully taken advantage of, would be to deprive the State of a large amount of income which the people of India had from time immemorial been accustomed to pay, and which, he said, " has all the authority of prescription and tradi-" tion in its favour; " an income which is drawn from the land, as has been observed by Mr. James Mill, " without any drain either upon the produce of any " man's labour, or the produce of any man's capital."

The objections that were raised to the redemption did not apply to a direct permanent settlement of the land revenue.

Great advantages were anticipated from such a measure; a general feeling of contentment would be diffused among all the landholders in the country, and they would, it was believed, become attached by the strongest ties of personal interest to the Government by which such a permanence was guaranteed to them, while great inducements would be given to them to lay out capital freely on the land, and to introduce improvements by which the wealth and prosperity of the country would be materially increased.

A permanent settlement would, in one respect, operate disadvantageously to the Government, inasmuch as it would cease to profit directly by any future augmentation of its income from this source; but it was the opinion of many men, well qualified to judge of such matters, that the Government could not fail indirectly to participate in any advantages accruing to its people, and that the people themselves would acquire more ability to bear increased taxation in other shapes. "Her Majesty's Government," wrote Sir Charles Wood to the Government of India, " entertain no doubt of the political advantages that " would attend a permanent settlement. The security, " and, it may almost be said, the absolute creation " of property in the soil which will flow from limita- " tion in perpetuity of the demands of the State on " the owners of land, cannot fail to stimulate or con- " firm their sentiments of attachment and loyalty to " the Government by whom so great a boon has been " conceded, and on whose existence its permanency " will depend."

A revision of the existing assessment was a necessary preliminary to a permanent settlement, and Sir Charles Wood directed that "a full, fair, and equable rent should be imposed on all lands under temporary settlement." He was prepared, after this was carried out, to sanction a permanent settlement of the land revenue throughout British India; at the same time desiring that the process of its introduction should be gradual, as it was impossible that establishments large enough for a general revision of the assessment could at once be provided.

Certain reservations in favour of the Government were directed to be made, whereby it might take advantage in participation hereafter of any mineral productions discovered in the soil, and of any improved culture resulting from the completion of schemes of irrigation in contemplation at the time of the settlement.

The summary settlement of enams,* chiefly in the presidencies of Madras and Bombay, including all tenures of land held under favourable conditions, has been vigorously prosecuted of late years; the old rules by which inquiry was instituted into a title on the decease of any holder having produced a vast amount of vexation and annoyance. Under the new regulations laid down in 1859, all these inquiries are set at rest, and inconvertible titles, and the option of converting their terminable tenure into freeholds, by the payment of a sum to Government, have been given to the holders of the enams.

A special department for the management of the extensive forests, and forest-lands of India, has been carefully organized, and experienced foresters have been sent from this country to assist in their conservation and superintendence; and the results in the supply of timber for railway purposes, as well as in an improvement in the climate of many districts by the replacement of trees, which had almost disappeared, will, doubtless, prove very great and beneficial.

The cultivation of the chinchona tree in India has been an object of great interest at home, and that interest has now been happily rewarded by the extraordinary success which has attended its introduction into that country. On the Neilgherry Hills acres and acres of land are now covered with plantations of these

* A gift or rent-free tenure.

beautiful trees, and Mr. Markham, who, with considerable danger to his health and life, originally superintended the removal of the plants from Peru to Madras in 1860, and to whom the credit of the experiment is principally due, had, on his second visit to India, in the autumn of 1865, the satisfaction of finding all the plantations flourishing, and upwards of a million of trees growing successfully.

Some idea of the value of the quinine can be formed from a remark made in Mr. Henry Waterfield's valuable statement, showing the moral and material progress of India in 1864-65, when he mentions the fact that, " independently of the great saving that will
" accrue from the possession of chinchona to the
" Indian Government, which has been estimated at
" not less than 50,000l. a year, for the supply of
" quinine to the troops alone, the result of the
" experiment is very satisfactory in having opened
" a vast field for the cultivation of this valuable
" plant, the best species of which appeared likely,
" ere long, to become almost extinct in South
" America, and in having demonstrated that the medi-
" cinal qualities of the bark are capable of con-
" siderable improvement under proper culture ; whilst
" it is impossible to calculate the value of the benefit
" bestowed upon the general population, by placing
" within their reach the fever-expelling preparations
" of the plant, which, from their high price, have
" hitherto been inaccessible to any but the wealthy
" classes."

CHAPTER IX.

PUBLIC WORKS.

How deeply Sir Charles Wood was impressed with the desire to improve the civil administration of India, and to accelerate the extension of reproductive public works, will be apparent, when it is remembered that, between the years 1862-3 and 1865-6, the annual expenditure on those heads was increased by nearly four millions per annum. There were, indeed, few subjects to which Sir Charles Wood devoted more constant consideration, than that of public works. Even when it was necessary to obtain repeated loans in order to meet the extraordinary expenditure caused by the mutiny, he was anxious to avoid any interruption of the progress of works for which an adequate supply of labour could be obtained.

A large expenditure was sanctioned and directed for the construction of roads in all parts of India, especially in the cotton districts, which will be adverted to hereafter.

Large sums of money were annually expended on the completion of the canals in the North-West Provinces and in the Punjab, and in the formation of the subsidiary channels necessary for the wider diffusion of their benefits.

The Ganges Canal, in 1860, had been of incalculable advantage to the famine-stricken people in the districts through which it passed, not only in irrigating land which, without its fertilizing waters, would have been barren wastes, but by bringing down grain from more favoured districts for the relief of the sufferers. In 1864, a report, drawn up by Captain Crofton, showed that a large outlay was required for remedying certain defects in the construction of the canal; and authority was given for effecting the needful repairs. It is believed that by this expenditure, estimated to amount to no less a sum than half a million, the canal will be rendered well adapted for irrigation, as well as navigation.

Money was also advanced for the improvement of the Eastern and Western Jumna Canals, which, as Colonel Baird Smith said in his able report on the famine and its causes in 1860-61, did noble work in watering during the famine very nearly half a million of acres, and thus supplying an amount of good grain very moderately estimated at about six and a half millions of bushels.

In the Madras Presidency the works necessary for the extension and completion of the great systems of irrigation in the deltas of the Godavery and Kistna, have been fully sanctioned.

That many, if not all these works, will prove essentially reproductive, as anticipated by Sir Charles Wood, when he authorized such an enormous and yearly increasing expenditure upon them, is shown by the beneficial results which have generally followed the construction of such works in India, and especially by the striking improvement in the value of property and in the condition of the people, in the extensive districts of the deltas of the Godavery and Kistna, in consequence of the restoration and extension of the old irrigation works connected with those rivers, and by the well-established success of the Jumna Canals in the North-Western Provinces.

In the year 1862, in addition to the current expenditure of the year, sanction was given by Sir Charles Wood for the employment of a sum amounting to 3,000,000*l*. from the cash balances for the further prosecution of reproductive works; and this money was not used, simply on the ground that sufficient labour was not obtainable to employ so vast a sum. In 1863-64 the amount to be applied to public works in India amounted to 5,237,200*l*., or, including the guaranteed interest on railways, to 9,237,200*l*.; but this was not all. "The Government," said Sir Charles Trevelyan, "desires that it may be clearly understood that any "funds that can be expended with advantage on cotton "roads, or works of irrigation or navigation, or on "any other useful works, will be granted during the "ensuing year. There will be no difficulty as far as "money is concerned."

During this large outlay on reproductive works for the development of the communications of the country, a new demand, to the extent of some millions, was made for providing additional and improved barrack accommodation for the increased number of European troops; for not only was their number in India more than double that for which accommodation had been provided before the mutiny, but the altered proportion of the European and native troops had called for a re-arrangement of the military posts throughout the country, while very few of the existing barracks were found equal to the requirements of modern sanitary science.

The heavy expenditure requisite for this purpose was freely sanctioned, caution being enjoined only that the stations should be carefully selected, and that more work should not be undertaken at one time than could be efficiently superintended and executed.

It was not only by the expenditure of money from the revenues of India that Sir Charles Wood encouraged the execution of works of public improvement; he was always ready to give all reasonable assistance to those who were prepared to invest their capital in such undertakings in that country.

A guarantee of 5 per cent. had been given by Lord Stanley to the Madras Irrigation Company, on a capital of 1,000,000*l.* for 25 years for the execution of an extensive scheme of irrigation works in certain parts of the Madras Presidency, but when soon after the commencement of the works, it became evident that this sum would be utterly insufficient for the completion of the project as originally designed, Sir Charles Wood entered into a contract with the Company under the conditions of which they confidently expected that they would be enabled to raise the requisite capital without the aid of a guarantee. Circumstances, connected to some extent with the unfavourable condition of the money market, have hitherto prevented the realization of these expectations, and the operations of the Company have, therefore, been restricted to that portion of their canal which is between Sunkasala and Cuddapah, and the Home Government have recently consented, on the application of the Company, to advance them the further sum of 600,000*l.*; a condition being, however, attached to the concession, viz., that, should the canal not be open by 1871, the works shall be made over to the Government for an amount of Indian stock equivalent to that which may have been laid out in their construction.

Large irrigation works on the Mahanuddy were entrusted to the East India Irrigation Company, who have already nearly completed a navigable canal from Balighat to Calcutta; and the execution of irrigation works in the Behar district, from the river Soane, on a plan proposed by Colonel Dickens of the Bengal Artillery, was also offered to the company.

No allusion has yet been made to railways and telegraphs—the two works which have tended more than any other to the consolidation of our power, and to the civilization and future peace and welfare of India. In June, 1859, the total length of rail open for traffic throughout the British dominions in India was 1,438 miles; at the commencement of 1866 the number of miles open for traffic was 3,332.

The recent opening of the bridge at Allahabad has brought within thirty-seven hours of each other

Calcutta, the capital of Eastern India, and Delhi, the ancient capital of the Moguls, which two cities are 1,000 miles apart; and, when the advantages likely to accrue from the improved facilities of communication for military purposes, as well as the impulse that is thus given to the commerce and trade of India, are considered, the taunt hurled in the teeth of the East India Company in 1783 cannot now be repeated, that " England has built no bridges, made no high roads, " cut no navigations, dug out no reservoirs. Every " other conqueror of every other description has left " some monument, either of state or beneficence, " behind him. Were we to be driven out of India " this day, nothing would remain to tell that it had " been possessed during the inglorious period of our " dominion by anything better than the ourang-outang " or the tiger." If in future years India shall cease to be a British possession, her railways alone will be sufficient proof that our rule was a beneficent one to the people.

Whether, therefore, we look to the development of railways as affecting the rapid concentration of troops, the carriage of merchandise, the ease and security of travellers, the facilities of personal intercourse, or the spread of intelligence afforded thereby, we cannot fail to see with gratitude the vast improvements they have wrought in the administration of Government and the amelioration of the social condition of the people.

The map of India was already covered by a complete network of lines of telegraph, before Sir Charles

Wood became Secretary of State; but during his tenure of office, the telegraph from England to India by the Persian Gulf was commenced, and under the able superintendence, and by the personal exertions, of Colonel Patrick Stewart, was brought to a successful issue; but, alas, at a heavy cost. He, who in his short life had undergone more dangers, braved more perils, and encountered more adventures than are often crowded into that of an old man, died of fever in the moment of his greatest triumph. Full of enterprise and zeal, beloved by all who knew him, Colonel Patrick Stewart had the satisfaction of knowing that he had nobly done his duty, and that his success had been appreciated and rewarded at home.

It was a remarkable achievement of science that led to the completion of telegraphic communication from India to England by a line surrounded with dangers of all kinds by land and by sea. From Kurrachee to Constantinople it extends for three thousand miles, half of its distance being submarine and half through unhealthy countries and desolate wastes. The working of this line, though at times messages have been passed through it with almost miraculous rapidity, has not been on the whole quite satisfactory; the fault, however, has not been due to the defective construction of the line, but to the many interruptions that have occurred, for the most part in countries not under the control of the English or Indian Governments.

CHAPTER X.

COTTON.

GREAT as had been the outlay on public works of late years, a demand for still greater outlay was raised, not only in India, but at home, during 1863, and Lancashire manufacturers called loudly for extravagant expenditure on cotton cultivation, without, perhaps, inquiring or knowing what had been already done, and what was then doing. Without considering the capabilities of India, or the tenure on which the land was held, or the position of the native ryots, they inveighed against Sir Charles Wood, because he did not consider that "India meant cotton, and cotton "meant India," but held that his duty, as Secretary of State, was to "govern India for the good of the "greatest number of the hundred and eighty millions "consigned to the care of England." *

---

* "The Manchester Chamber of Commerce have raised a cry "against a minister who has refused to concede its preposterous "demands, but Sir Charles Wood knows that his business is not "with Manchester, but with India. His sphere is not a narrow one, "bounded by the walls of Cottonopolis, but a wide one, extending "from the Himalayas to Cape Comorin, and peopled with one "hundred and eighty millions of human beings. Mr. Hugh Mason, "a member of the Chamber, has been pleased to declare that India "means cotton, and cotton means India; but Sir Charles Wood

It was painful to any liberal politician to watch how the influence of personal interests eclipsed in the minds of many of the cotton manufacturers the leading principles of free trade, which were entirely lost sight of, in nearly all the suggestions that were made in respect to the supply of cotton from India.

It will not be out of place to see what had been done for the furtherance of the growth of cotton in India, and its transport to this country. It was constantly alleged that the want of roads and difficulty of transit were so great that it was impossible to convey cotton to the ports for shipment; that nothing had been done or attempted to be done by the Government of India to obviate these difficulties; that a contract law, with penal clauses, was necessary; that there should be special interference with the ryots to compel them to grow cotton; that all land on which cotton was grown should be exempted from payment of rent for two years; that, finally, Government should make itself the medium between the producer and manufacturer, and buy the cotton at a fixed price, thus in fact entering the lists as a cotton broker.

The question no doubt was deserving of all attention. Nor did it fail to receive it. The wants of

"believes that cotton, though a good thing—and one which might be
"grown here, not by Government, but by private enterprise—is not
"the highest good of India. Sir Charles Wood believes, and this
"meeting is a living proof that the people of this country share in
"this belief, that India means good government, enlightened legis-
"lation, and the moral and mental elevation of its myriad millions."
—Speech of *Baboo Kissory Chand Mittra*, at a public meeting at Calcutta, 7th March, 1863.

Lancashire invested it with no common feelings of anxiety, and afforded some excuse for the thoughtless clamour indulged in by some of the manufacturers in that county.

But the subject of the growth of American cotton was not a new one in India. As long ago as 1843 experimental farms for its cultivation were formed by the East India Company in different parts of the country, and when, by the success of these experiments, the capability of growing American cotton in India had been established, supplies of fresh seeds were distributed to the ryots, and, in order to give ample encouragement to them, the Directors of the East India Company undertook to buy all cotton of a certain quality at a fixed price. By these means they proved India's capacity to grow American cotton, but it was for the consumer and not the Government to decide whether its production should be encouraged and increased by such a price as would induce the natives of India to cultivate it. The British merchants did not offer the price required, and, as a natural and certain consequence, the growth of the superior kinds of cotton fell off, and the producers grew only that material which was best suited to their own or the China market.

Lord Dalhousie, on his annexation of Nagpore, had seen the importance of the cotton question. "The pos-
" session of that country," he wrote, " will materially
" aid in supplying a want, upon the secure supply of
" which much of the manufacturing prosperity of
" England depends."

In the early part of 1861, before the commencement of the American war, Lord Canning, seeing the probability of a rupture between the north and south in the United States, and anticipating the certainty of a greatly and suddenly increased demand for Indian cotton in England, published a resolution drawing the attention of the local governments to measures for meeting the demand that was likely to arise.

All information on the subject was to be collected from public records, and, when obtained, was to be freely distributed all over the country to producers. The demand likely to occur in England, and the ruling prices, were also rapidly to be communicated to them.

Agents of the mercantile community were invited to visit the cotton-producing districts. The Government offered the aid of the public treasuries in the interior to capitalists in their banking arrangements; an official inspection of country cart and bullock tracks was ordered; and an offer was made to pay the expenses of any gentlemen connected with the trade who would accompany the officers so employed, and "observe " and report on any obstacles other than physical " which may appear to impede the cotton trade."

Handbooks on the cultivation of cotton in India were compiled in each presidency, and prizes of 1,000*l.* in Bengal, Madras, and Bombay were offered for the largest quantity of cotton combined with the best quality grown on any one estate.

These measures were all sanctioned and generally approved of by Sir Charles Wood.

In July of the same year the Manchester Cotton Supply Association deputed Mr. Haywood, their secretary, to proceed to India. The services of Dr. Forbes, superintendent of the Dharwar Cotton Gin Factory, who was in England at the time, were at once placed by Sir Charles Wood at the disposal of the company. Mr. Haywood, however, on his arrival in India, refused to buy any cotton. The people, believing that he had come to purchase, flocked round him, offering even to keep their cotton till his return from upper India; but his authority to purchase for the company had been withdrawn, if ever granted, before he touched the shores of India.

Indeed, the affairs of the association seem to have been sadly mismanaged at Sedashagur. While the agents of Bombay houses were active and busy, making the most of all available means, buying land, building sheds and boats, setting up steam-mills and cotton presses, the agents of the association were watching valuable machinery rusting on the shore, and doing little more than constructing an office with expensive materials imported from England!

The most pressing orders were sent by Sir Charles Wood for the construction of a road up the Khyga Ghaut, to Dharwar, and a large body of workmen were collected on the spot; but fever seized upon the labourers with a virulence which killed many, weakened more, and drove away the rest in fear and panic. No inducement that could be offered would tempt them to return to what they imagined certain death. In this state of things a road was commenced over the Arbyle Ghaut, and within a few months was opened to within half a mile of Sedashagur, and this road was completed before the cotton-presses from England had been set up.

The energetic Governor of Bombay, Sir Bartle Frere, himself visited the fever-stricken districts. " Almost " every man," he wrote, "that we met had been, or " was when we saw him, fever-stricken, and, from the " miserable emaciated figures, and enlarged spleens of " the poor wretches, I can well believe the tales we " were told of its ravages among the wild, ill-fed, ill-" clothed people of these forest tracts. It seems to " strike terror into every class, especially the work-" men, who abscond after a few day's stay, and cannot " now be got to engage at all on the ghaut works."

It was not, however, only for the construction of roads for the conveyance of cotton that labour was deficient; the crops could not be properly got in from the same cause. In Berar, the great cotton-field of India, said Dr. Forbes, " manual labour is still more " scanty. The produce, as it is picked from the field, " is piled up in one large heap in the open air, where " it remains sometimes for months, until labour can be " obtained. Although the cultivation of native cotton " is capable of extension to an enormous degree, yet " the amount of manual labour available is barely " sufficient to clean the quantity now produced; any " large extension without the aid of cleaning ma-" chinery, therefore, cannot be expected; and this " remark is the more applicable, when it is considered " that the chief increase of cotton cultivation must be

" looked for in new districts, such as those of Central
" India, where population is thin and scarcely suffi-
" cient to till the land."

Mr. Stanborough, who was for some time settled in Berar, reported that the amount of labour employed on the railroads and construction of roads seriously interfered with the cultivation of cotton : indeed, a similar complaint of the scarcity of labourers was received from all parts of India.

The Government, however, did not relax its efforts for facilitating the conveyance of cotton from the fields of production.

In the year 1861-2 more than half a million of money was applied, out of a total expenditure on public works of 4,742,183l., for the purposes of facilitating the conveyance of cotton. In Bengal the able Lieutenant-Governor, Sir John Peter Grant, devoted much time to the construction of roads, which enabled the cotton of Singboom to be conveyed to the Grand Trunk Road and to the railway. In the following years not much less than half a million has been annually expended on cotton roads alone.

In the Madras Presidency the Godavery had been surveyed with a view to its being created a navigable river many years ago, and numerous plans and estimates had been framed, but no operations on a large scale were begun until the year 1861. As a matter of emergency, in the cotton famine of 1862 an attempt was made to surmount the obstacles formed by the three great rocky barriers, by temporarily constructed tramways being made at the points where the stream was unnavigable, by which means goods passing down the river were transported on carts beyond the rapids; but this necessity for breaking bulk proved very inconvenient and expensive. In 1863, therefore, the entire force of labour that could be obtained was thrown on the completion of the works in the river, which were ordered to be pushed on as rapidly as possible: the object being the rapid transmission of cotton from the plateau of Berar to the seaboard—a line of navigation upwards of three hundred miles in length, over which it is hoped that, after the completion of the works, boats will be enabled to pass during six months in the year. The same dispersion of the labourers, however, from fever, which occurred in Canara, was also experienced in these works.

The cotton-fields of Berar and Surat are now penetrated by the Great Indian Peninsula, and the Bombay and Baroda Railways. Before this, cotton from the former district had to be carried to the port of Bombay, a distance of 450 or 500 miles, on the backs of bullocks, whose average pace was one mile per hour, or in small country carts. Had the American war found India less provided with internal means of rapid communication, Lancashire would have been deprived of her best source of mitigating the calamity which fell so heavily upon her; and, notwithstanding the impetus given to the cotton-trade by increased price, it would have been impossible that the exports of that article could have increased, as they actually did, from 1,717,240 cwts. in 1859 to 4,911,843 cwts.

in 1863-4, while, even after the cessation of hostilities in the United States, they were not less than 4,663,808 cwts. in 1864-5.

"We have no want of means," said Sir Bartle Frere, the Governor of Bombay, "nor of encourage-"ment from the Government of India, or from the "Secretary of State, to do our duty by the country; "not only have they sanctioned all that we could "show was required, but in all their communications "they have not ceased to urge on us the necessity for "making due provision for the wants of the cotton-"trade."

Great complaints were made in England about the inferior quality and adulteration of Surat cotton, which was no doubt bad; but this arose in great part from the system of purchase encouraged by the European merchants, almost holding out a premium for fraud. The price given was for quantity, not quality.

In the warehouses of Dharwar a regular system of cotton adulteration existed; on one side of the sheds was a heap of Dharwar cotton of superior growth, on the other a heap of dirty and inferior cotton to be mixed with it; but this was not all: stones, rubbish, the sweepings of warehouses, and refuse of every description, were promiscuously mingled together; and thus, if the quality was deteriorated, the quantity and weight were unmistakably increased.

The only step which the Government could take to prevent the adulteration of the staple was to pass an Act punishing fraudulent adulterations with heavy penalties; and a law to effect this was enacted in

Bombay, which to a large extent prevented such dishonest practices.

All having been done that was legitimate on the part of a Government, and perhaps a little more, in furtherance of the growth and export of cotton, the rest was wisely left to private enterprise, and to those unfailing laws which govern supply and demand; and the increase in the amount of cotton received from India has justified the expectation that to those laws might safely be left the encouragement of its production.

CHAPTER XI.

EDUCATION.

WHILE the measures for the material improvement of the people of India engrossed so much of Sir Charles Wood's time, their mental and moral welfare was by no means neglected.

It is impossible to speak of the progress of education during the last seven years, without referring to the despatch of the Court of Directors in 1854, which was prepared under Sir Charles Wood's directions, and which has ever since been considered as the charter of education in India.

In words which read almost like the commencement of a paraphrase of Dr Johnson's celebrated epitaph on Goldsmith, it was said by a speaker in the House of Lords, " that it had left no part of the " question of education in India untouched, and it " dealt with every branch of the subject judiciously " and effectually."

In that elaborate document a plan was laid down, complete in all its parts from the highest to the lowest, from the enlarged system of university and collegiate education down to the poor village schools; and, as Lord Dalhousie said, " it left nothing to be desired,

" if indeed it did not authorise and direct that more
" should be done than is within our present grasp."

In accordance with the instructions contained in that despatch, educational departments were formed in every Presidency and every Lieutenant-Governorship, and inspectors and other officers were attached to those departments.

The London University was taken as the model on which the establishment of the universities was to be framed, due allowance being made for the various conditions of the inhabitants of India, differing so widely as they do from one another in many important particulars.

Professorships, for the delivery of lectures on subjects of science, were instituted in connection with the universities, and special degrees were awarded for proficiency in the vernacular languages, as well as Sanskrit, Arabic, and Persian.

The schools for the education of natives throughout the length and breadth of British India required some assistance, not only for their establishment, but for their maintenance when established. Anxious, however, as Sir Charles Wood was to provide that " useful and practical knowledge suited to every sta-" tion in life should be conveyed to the great mass " of the people who were utterly incapable of " obtaining any education worthy of the name by " their own unaided efforts," he felt that, while granting additional sums for the purpose, the Government resources were inadequate alone to carry out so large a scheme of education of the natives as he contemplated, and he desired, moreover, to enlist as much as possible the interests and exertions of the natives themselves in favour of education. He therefore determined to found the general education in India on the basis of grants in aid to all schools, irrespective of the religious opinions of those who promoted or conducted them, and to observe an entire abstinence from interference with the religious instruction conveyed in the schools assisted. Thus were the spontaneous efforts of the people in the cause of education fostered and encouraged, with the assistance of considerably increased expenditure from the revenue.

It will be obvious to all who are acquainted with India, how important it was that this question of religious instruction should be properly settled, if any general extension of education was to be effected.

The co-operation of the natives could not be expected unless their religious feelings and prejudices were respected, and, on the other hand, it was necessary to avoid alienating the Christian teachers and missionaries by whom some of the best and most efficient of the schools in India were conducted.

The question was agitated with great eagerness how far the Bible should be introduced into Government schools, and whether clergymen should be employed in the educational department.

Both these points were happily settled by adopting the principle acted on in the Irish system of education, of not allowing religious instruction to be given as part of the system of the Government schools, and of making grants in aid to all schools, Christian, Mahomedan, or Hindoo.

The Bible was placed in the libraries of all the Government schools, and instruction in the Bible, and in the tenets and doctrines of Christianity, was allowed to be given to all pupils at their own request, and in any manner most convenient, out of school hours.

Without any unnecessary interference with the freedom of individual thought and private views, it was laid down as an inviolable rule that no person in the service of the Government should make use of the influence of his position under Government for the purpose of proselytism. In a few cases, clergymen possessed of special qualifications were employed as professors, but they were not generally allowed to act as inspectors of schools. Sir Charles Wood had consulted officers of the Government who had the greatest experience and knowledge of the natives, and also some of the ablest of the conductors of the missionary establishments; and he had come to the firm conviction " that the extension of the Christian religion in India " must be left to the voluntary efforts of individuals and " societies, and that the interference of Government " would tend, by inflaming the religious prejudices of " the natives, to check, rather than promote this " object."

More than once had he emphatically to lay down the principle enunciated so clearly and impartially in the despatch of 1854, and confirmed by Lord Stanley's despatch of 1859, that religious instruction must be sought by the pupils of their own free will; that the giving, as well as receiving, instruction must be equally voluntary; that it must be given out of school hours, so as not to interfere in any way with the course of instruction in the schools; and that it should not be noticed by the inspectors in their periodical visits.

By these rules, openly avowed, and strictly adhered to, Sir Charles Wood, without yielding to the views of either extreme party in this country, secured alike the respect and co-operation of all parties in England and India; and during his tenure of office no religious animosities, so often fatal to the cause of religion itself, were raised or perpetuated.

Large funds for the promotion of education were provided from native resources; and, as regards the Government expenditure, Sir Charles Wood was firmly convinced that whatever was incurred would, in the words of Sir Thomas Munro, so appropriately used at the conclusion of his despatch, "be amply repaid by "the improvement of the country; for the general "diffusion of knowledge is inseparably followed by "more orderly habits, by increasing industry, by a "taste for the comforts of life, by exertions to acquire "them, and by the growing prosperity of the country."

The grant-in-aid system, inaugurated in 1854, has been successful beyond all expectation, the voluntary donations of the people being met by contributions of equal value on the part of the Government, while the outlay on education generally has been amply provided for and increased.

Since 1859 there has been little to do but to watch with pleasure and satisfaction the progress of education, under the principles laid down in the despatch of 1854. Candidates for the universities, as well as those who have taken degrees, have increased rapidly in number, and the admission of the pupils to the various colleges and schools throughout India has been on a greatly augmented scale.

In Madras an Act was passed empowering villages to tax themselves for the support of schools; and the example may probably lead to similar efforts being made in other parts of India.

In 1861-2 the expenditure from the public revenue was 322,593*l*., and in the budget estimate of 1866-67 no less than 763,230*l*. has been allotted to this purpose.

Notwithstanding the deep-rooted prejudices existing in India against female education, the number of girls under instruction has largely increased. Mr. Drinkwater Bethune, when Legislative Member of Council, and President of the Council of Education at Calcutta, had given every encouragement to the formation of female schools throughout British India, and he established one in that city for girls, the children of natives of wealth and rank. His exertions in the cause were cordially seconded by Lord Dalhousie, who, on Mr. Bethune's death in 1851, adopted and supported the school, until his departure from India, when, so impressed was he with its importance, that he recorded his high opinion of the institution in terms which induced the home authorities to undertake from that time its entire pecuniary maintenance. There are now, however, other causes at work tending to the same desirable end, and the augmented number of pupils may be immediately attributed, says the director of public instruction in Bengal, " to the growing " influence of the young men, who have received the " full advantages of a high university education in " the different colleges throughout the country."

At Lahore, Sir Robert Montgomery, the able Lieutenant-Governor of the Punjab, held an educational durbar in 1865, and received deputations from the native chiefs and gentry, of the Mahomedan, Hindoo, and Sikh creeds, anxious to develope further the education of young women, and offering as a tribute and proof of their sincerity in the cause, an annual sum towards the scheme, in the hope that the future mothers of their chiefs and owners of the land might be capable of rearing a race of enlightened sons, who, by their education and advanced civilization, should be able to take their proper places in the administration of the affairs of their native country.

Amongst the supporters of the movement Sir Robert Montgomery mentions Baba Khan Sing, the most revered gooroo, or religious teacher, in the Punjab, of noble descent, who has himself established 75 schools, attended by 1,172 girls, increasing the total number now under instruction to 9,000.

In 1863 a scheme of general education for the province of Oude, prepared by the Chief Commissioner, Mr. Wingfield, was sanctioned. In its leading features it was similar to those which have been introduced with so much success in other districts of India, and will probably be found to afford sufficient scope for the action of the local administration for some years to come.

The talookdars of Oude, anxious to perpetuate their grateful remembrance of Lord Canning, have instituted, at Lucknow, a college to be called after his name, in which a separate department is constituted where the children of the chiefs and principal landowners of the province may receive their education; but the college will also be thrown open to the natives of the country generally. An annual grant, equal in amount to the endowment of the talookdars, will be made by Government.

The rich merchants of Bombay, following the noble example of enlightened liberality set before them by Sir Jamsetjee Jejeebhoy, whose gifts to, and endowments of, charitable and educational institutions in Bombay during twenty years amounted to upwards of 200,000*l.*, have largely contributed to various similar objects. Mr. David Sassoon's name will long be remembered in connection with a reformatory established by him; Mr. Rustomjee Jamsetjee Jejeebhoy has offered 10,000*l.* for the promotion of English education in Guzerat and Bombay, besides, in conjunction with his brothers, spending 1,200*l.* on the School of Arts in the Presidency town.

Large contributions have been given by Mr. Chesetjee Furdonjee to the foundation of a school at Surat; Mr. Premchund Roychund has placed at the disposal of the Government 1,200*l.* and a house for a girls' school; while Mr. Mungaldas Nathabhoy has founded a travelling fellowship for Hindoos in the

Bombay University, at a cost of 2,000*l*., and has endowed a professorship of economic science, as well as provided funds for building the Civil Engineering College at Poona.

Whether, therefore, we look to these generous and magnificent donations, to the increased interest shown in education by the chiefs in Oude and the Punjab, or to the appreciation of these advantages manifested by the poorer natives, and the readiness evinced, in many quarters, to come forward in support of the schools, we cannot but believe that, under the blessing of God, we have good grounds for satisfaction for the present, and hope for the future.

CHAPTER XII.

POLITICAL.

WHEN Sir Charles Wood entered upon his duties as Secretary of State for India, the mutiny and rebellion of 1857-58 had been trampled out; but it still remained for the British Government, by a wise and generous policy, to restore confidence to the princes and nobles of the land, and to render permanent the peace which, in the first instance, had been accomplished by the strength and valour of our arms. As our enemies had been punished, so were our friends to be rewarded. This good work Lord Canning was pushing forward with congenial energy; and he was warmly supported by Sir Charles Wood, who addressed letters to many of our most faithful friends and adherents, thanking them in the name of the Queen, for the good services, "more precious than gold and silver," which they had rendered to the British Government. Throughout his administration, Sir Charles Wood has scrupulously abstained from aggression or annexation; what is known as the adoption policy of Lord Canning was cordially accepted by him; and in reply to the Governor-General's despatch on this important subject, he wrote:—"It is not by the extension of our empire that its permanence is to be secured, but by the character of British rule in the territories already committed to our care, and by practically demonstrating that we are as willing to respect the rights of others, as we are capable of maintaining our own."

While such sentiments pervaded the minds of the authorities both in London and at Calcutta, it is not surprising that nothing has occurred to mar the perfect tranquillity which has prevailed within the limits of India since 1859.

The only occasions on which British troops have been called into action were three affairs on the frontier; the first in Sikkim, the second at the Umbeyla Pass, and the third in Bhootan. "With regard to these frontier raids," as Lord Dalhousie said in his memorable minute summing up the political events that had occurred, the measures that were taken, and the progress made during the course of his administration, "they are and must for the present be viewed as events inseparable from the state of society which for centuries past has existed among the mountain tribes. They are no more to be regarded as interruptions to the general peace in India than the street brawls which appear among the every-day proceedings of a police-court in London are regarded as indications of the existence of civil war in England."

The cases referred to form no exception to Lord Dalhousie's principle.

At the end of the year 1860 the outrages committed on British subjects by the Rajah of Sikkim and his minister compelled the Government of India to send a force into that country, in order to obtain satisfaction for the injuries which had been inflicted. In sanctioning this expedition, Sir Charles Wood expressed his cordial approval of the instructions given to the political officer, that a strict line should be drawn between the ruler, whose offensive conduct demanded reprisals, and the inhabitants of the country, to whom all possible consideration was to be shown. The military operations were brought to a successful close; the just punishment of the minister was obtained; and a treaty was negotiated, providing for free commercial intercourse with and through the country. "Her Majesty's Government," wrote Sir Charles Wood to Lord Canning, "hope that the
" moderation evinced by your declared intention not
" to annex any portion of the Sikkim territory to the
" British empire, will contribute as much to the main-
" tenance of a lasting peace, as it did to the speedy
" conclusion of the war."

In 1863 another expedition was undertaken to repress the marauding incursions of Mahomedan freebooters on the North-western frontier. Some of the fanatical Mahomedan tribes on the border, taking alarm at the approach of our troops, opposed their progress, but after some resistance they were signally defeated, and, finding what was the real object of our advance, several of their chiefs, at the instance of Major James, whose influence over them was very great, joined our troops in person, and conducted them to the stronghold of the marauders, which however was found to have been evacuated and destroyed before their arrival.

Shortly afterwards, the long-continued robberies of the Bhooteas, and ultimately their gross ill-treatment of a British envoy who had been sent to them in the hope of averting the necessity of hostile operations which had been contemplated by Lord Canning, rendered it imperative on the Indian Government to vindicate the honour of England, and take some security for their better behaviour in the future. The military operations were of a very trivial nature, and were brought to a close by a treaty, concluded with the Bhootan Rajas, the passes in the mountains through which the plundering expeditions issued on the plain having been placed in the hands of the British authorities.

While, then, the arm of the Government has not been slow to defend its subjects against attack from without, instances have not been wanting in which states under British rule have been restored to their native princes, and rights have been confirmed to native chiefs, in a spirit of liberality well calculated to increase our power.

In 1861 Kolapoor, which had been in the hands of the British Government since the suppression of the insurrection in 1845, was restored to the management of the Rajah, a young man twenty-seven years of age, anxious to assume the control of the affairs of his native country. In 1864 the administration of the principality of Dhar, which had been confiscated on account of the rebellion of its mercenary troops in the troubles of 1857, was restored to the Rajah. It had been Lord Stanley's intention, when in office, to have effected this restoration, but the age, inexperience, and incapacity of the young Rajah prevented its being concluded before 1864.

Sir Charles Wood's tenure of office has not, however, been destitute of political questions of grave importance, one of which—his grant to the Mahomedan princes of Mysore in 1859-60—created much comment and dissatisfaction in India.

After the death of Tippoo Saib at the storming of Seringapatam in 1799, these princes and their families had been removed to Vellore, and an allowance of about 77,000*l*. per annum was settled upon them. Their supposed complicity in the Vellore mutiny in 1806 entailed upon them their removal to Calcutta, and the forfeiture of any claim on the British Government. They lived in seclusion at Russapugla, under the superintendence of a British officer, and were treated as royal pensioners by the Indian Government; but the profligacy and the disreputable course of life pursued by several of them tended neither to their advantage nor honour, nor to that of the Government.

In this state of things, Sir Charles Wood was very anxious that the settlement should be broken up and the Mysore stipendiaries absorbed in the general mass of the people. He was desirous to place them in a better position as regarded their own independence and power of utility; and, at the same time, to relieve the Government of India from the charge of a numerous and increasing body of pensioners. He proposed therefore to allow each member of the family to settle where he pleased away from Calcutta, free from any Government supervision; and, in order to place this in their power, he proposed to create an amount of India stock, the interest of which should make provision for their incomes. The sum allotted for their permanent provision amounted to 17,000*l.* per annum for their lives. An equal amount was assigned to the existing heads of families for their lives, and a certain sum was granted for the purchase of houses elsewhere than in Calcutta. The whole provision was very far below the sum originally set apart for their maintenance, or the interest of the sum which had accrued to the Government by withholding part of it for so many years.

"When I review," says Sir Charles Wood in his despatch of the 4th of February, 1861, " all the circum-
" stances of British relations with the families of Hyder
" Ali and Tippoo Sultan, from the time of the conquest
" of Mysore; when I advert to the terms of the treaty
" of 1799,—to the revenues of the territory assigned
" for the maintenance of the family; when I consider
" the intentions of the framers of the treaty, the
" recorded opinions of Lord Wellesley, and especially
" of the Duke of Wellington, who remonstrated
" against the illiberal manner in which effect was given
" to a treaty he helped to negotiate; when I refer to
" the accounts of the ' appropriated Mysore Deposit

" 'Fund,' and know that in the year 1806, when neither
" of the contingencies contemplated in the treaty as
" grounds for a reduction of the payments to the
" family had occurred, there were accumulations to
" the credit of the fund greater than the amounts
" which I have ordered to be distributed amongst
" existing members of the family; when I consider
" that since that time the sums actually paid to the
" descendants of Hyder Ali and Tippoo Sultan fell
" short of those specified in the treaty by a larger
" amount than that which I have ordered to be
" capitalized, as a permanent provision for the family;
" that the annual amount now paid to existing incum-
" bents is below that stated in the treaty; and that,
" on the death of these incumbents, many of whom
" are of advanced age, the territories assigned for
" the maintenance of the family will revert to the
" British Government in perpetuity, free from all
" charge or incumbrance; and when I bear in mind
" the claims of a body of men, descended from a
" sovereign prince, to generous sympathy and bene-
" ficent treatment, and the benefit which they will
" derive from being placed in a position of honourable
" independence, I cannot think that the demands of
" justice and humanity would have been satisfied by
" any less liberal arrangement than that which has
" been directed by her Majesty's Government."

Another question of a similar nature, which had more than once been discussed in Parliament, was Azeem Jah's claim to be recognized as the titular Nawab of the Carnatic. In the early wars during the last century with the French, the ancestor of Azeem Jah, Mahomed Ali, one of the pretenders to the Nawabship, was our ally, and his claim was supported by the English, as that of his rival was by the French. On the ultimate victory of the English, he was rewarded by being established as the independent sovereign of the Carnatic. In 1795 Mahomed Ali was succeeded by his son, Omdut ul Omrah. At the time, however, of Tippoo Saib's most violent hostility to the British Government, the Nawabs, both father and son, forgetting the obligations by which they should have been bound, entered into correspondence with him; and proofs were discovered at the capture of Seringapatam, which satisfied Lord Wellesley, and the ablest men at the time in India, of their treachery.

On the death of Omdut ul Omrah, which almost immediately ensued, in 1801, Azeem ul Dowlah was placed on the throne, and a treaty was signed with him, in the same year, by which a certain income and certain privileges were assured to him for life; the British Government "remaining at " liberty to exercise its rights, founded on the faith-" less policy of its ally, in whatever manner might " be deemed most conducive to the immediate safety, " and to the general interests of the Company in the " Carnatic. Thus," said Lord Dalhousie in his minute of the 19th of December, 1855, " in 1801 the terri-" tories of the Nawab of the Carnatic were at the " absolute disposal of the British Government."

In 1819 Azeem ul Dowlah died, and his son, Azeem Jah, was recognized as his successor. On the death of the latter, in 1825, his infant son, Mahomed Ghouse, succeeded, and during his minority his affairs were conducted by his uncle Azeem Jah, the term of whose administration was rendered conspicuous by an exhausted exchequer, enormous debts, hideous profligacy, and fraudulent proceedings tending " to bring high " station to disrepute, and favouring the accumulation " of an idle and dissipated population in the chief " city of the presidency."

On the death of Mahomed Ghouse, without children, in 1855, the friends of Azeem Jah in this country, founding their pretensions on the treaty of 1801, claimed for him the Nawabship of the Carnatic, and its rights and dignities, as hereditary. Lord Harris and Lord Dalhousie both refused to place Azeem Jah on the throne; the Home Government, when Mr. Vernon Smith was President of the Board of Control, confirmed their decision; but again and again was Sir Charles Wood pressed to confer the sovereignty on Azeem Jah.

Had he consented, he would have reversed the decision of Lord Clive, Lord Wellesley, Lord Dalhousie and Lord Harris, and would have entailed on India the mischief of more royal puppets, whose ancestral names and dynastic traditions made them often the rallying points of disaffection and treason. Sir Charles Wood firmly, and more than once, resisted these appeals, founded, as they were, on erroneous grounds and inaccurate statements.

The members of the late Mahomed Ghouse's immediate family had been already liberally provided for, and Sir Charles Wood increased Prince Azeem Jah's allowance to 15,000*l.* a year; consenting to recognize his position as that of " the first nobleman " of the Carnatic."

The most important political question which arose during Sir Charles Wood's tenure of office was, whether the administration of the affairs of Mysore, of which the Rajah had been deprived in the year 1834, should be restored to him.

About a hundred years ago, Mysore was an independent state, under the rule of a Hindoo Rajah. Hyder Ali, a Mahomedan adventurer in the service of the Rajah, deposed his master and usurped the government of the country, which he conducted with great ability. He was succeeded, in 1782, by his son Tippoo Saib, whose inveterate hostility to the British Government was only terminated by his death at the capture of Seringapatam and the conquest of Mysore in 1799. Part of the territory of Mysore ruled over by these Mahomedan princes was taken possession of by the British Government, part was assigned to the Nizam, who had been the ally of the English during the war. The remainder, with some additional territory, was formed into a separate state, and a young child, a descendant of the old Rajahs of Mysore, was taken from prison, and placed in possession of it, the arrangements being sanctioned in a treaty concluded between the British Government and the Nizam. From this treaty the Rajah's title is derived. In addition to this, a treaty was made with the Rajah, called the Subsidiary Treaty of Mysore, which contained the relations and defined the conditions which were to subsist between the British Government and the Rajah. It was stipulated that a certain annual sum should be paid to defray the expense of an auxiliary force, and, in default of payment, territory might be taken as security. The Rajah bound himself to be guided by the advice of the British Government, and provision was also made for "assuming " the management and collection of the said terri- " tories, as the Governor-General in Council shall " judge most expedient, for the purpose of securing " the efficiency of the said military funds, and of " providing for the effectual protection of the country " and the welfare of the people."

During the minority of the Rajah, the administration of the country was most efficiently carried on for several years by Purneah, a valuable Hindoo minister; but, upon the Rajah's accession to power, he was dismissed, the Rajah assuming to himself the Government. Under the Rajah's management affairs were so ill conducted, and such disorder prevailed over the whole country, that in 1831 the people rose in rebellion. In consequence of this state of things Lord William Bentinck, in 1834, moved a considerable body of English troops into the country, restored tranquillity by force of arms, and found himself under the necessity of assuming the administration of the country, in which state it has continued ever since, a large annual allowance, as stipulated by the treaty, being placed at the disposal of the Rajah.

Before he left India, Lord William Bentinck proposed to restore to the Rajah the greater part of the territories of Mysore. The Home Government, observing that, if the Rajah's character was sufficiently good to enable him to govern any of his territories well, there was little reason for not restoring the whole to him, expressed their opinion that his vices were permanent, and they desired the administration of the whole country to be retained till a good system of Government was established, and security taken for its continuance. Lord Auckland, in communicating the decision of the Home Government to the Rajah, stated that " the administration of his Highness's territories " should remain on its present footing until the " arrangements for their good government should have " been so firmly established as to be secure from " future disturbance."

The Rajah applied for a reversal of this decision to Sir Henry Hardinge, when he became Governor-General in 1844, who, avoiding any direct opinion on the subject of his restoration, desired the Commissioner to furnish an account of the Mysore debt to the British Government.

Again did the Rajah appeal, to Lord Canning. This appeal was made in 1861. In March, 1862, Lord Canning, after long and patient consideration of the request, informed the Rajah of his inability to " recog- " nize his claim, or to admit the claim on which it was " founded." He referred, in the course of a long despatch, to Sir Mark Cubbon's testimony, that any improvement that had taken place in Mysore had been effected in spite of the counteraction he had met with on the part of the Rajah and his adherents, and that his conduct during his suspension from power offered no security that the crisis which induced that suspension would not recur in the event of his restoration. Nothing could be clearer or more emphatic than Lord Canning's treatment of the question. He denied that a pledge of restoration was ever given, and declared that the Rajah had forfeited the administration of his country by his misconduct, and that the British Government intended to remain free to act as circumstances might render advisable.

The Rajah of Mysore, on the receipt of this despatch, renewed his appeal to Lord Elgin, who replied that "its allegations and reasonings did not " shake his confidence in the propriety of the decision " of his predecessors."

The protest and appeal of the Rajah were referred home to the Secretary of State in Council, and on him rested the final decision in this important case.

On referring to the opinion of successive Governor-Generals, Sir Charles Wood found that Lord Hardinge, Lord Dalhousie, Lord Canning, and Lord Elgin, supported by the valuable opinion of Sir Mark Cubbon, the chief commissioner in Mysore, had all expressed their views against the restoration of the administration of Mysore into the hands of the Rajah. To these views Sir Charles Wood naturally attributed much weight; but to Lord Canning's especially he attached great importance. "The name of Lord Canning," said he, in his despatch supporting the opinion given by Lord Elgin and the Indian Government, "will for

"ever be associated in the history of British India
"with the most liberal policy towards the native
"Princes of India. That lamented statesman has
"given abundant proof, not only that questions
"affecting their rights received from him a fair and
"impartial consideration, but that he cherished a
"lively sympathy with their feelings and interests,
"and his opinion therefore deserves especial con-
"sideration upon the present question."

Sir Charles Wood was averse to cancel the deliberate opinions of so many high authorities, and, taking into consideration the interests of the people of the country, long accustomed to the enlightened rule of the British Government, which they had learnt sincerely to appreciate and to respect, he refused to sanction the dangerous experiment of removing the administration out of the hands of British officers by whom the country had been so materially benefited.

The Rajah, having since adopted a distant relative, the power of adopting an heir to his title and his private property has been admitted; but no authority to adopt an heir to the raj of Mysore has ever been conceded to him, and he has been distinctly informed by the present Governor-General, Sir John Lawrence, that no such concession would now be made.

In the political troubles of Affghanistan Sir Charles Wood has consistently refused to bear a part, or to take any action beyond affording in British territory an asylum for refugees, and acknowledging the *de facto* rulers of that distracted country. He has thus set an example of non-interference with foreign politics, which has of late years been happily followed in this country.

It was Sir Charles Wood's good fortune to introduce into India a new order of knighthood to be conferred alike on distinguished Europeans and distinguished natives. Its title is the Star of India, and its motto, "Heaven's light our guide."

Never since Englishmen first conquered India has any decoration peculiar to that country been bestowed upon its native princes. Doubtless the conflicting elements of many creeds, the jealousies of caste, and the rivalries of race, had deterred any Governor-General or any government from making an experiment likely to be attended with so many difficulties.

It was reserved for Sir Charles Wood to be the first to obtain the sanction of the Crown to this new honour. More than a formal sanction was promptly accorded by the Queen. The Prince Consort himself took an active and energetic interest in the details of a measure which proved successful in overcoming all prejudices, jealousies, and heartburnings in India. Lord Canning added lustre to the order as its first grand master, and it is now worn with pride by the present Governor-General, the Nizam, Lord Gough, Sir George Pollock, the Maharajahs of Cashmere, Gwalior, and Indore, Sir George Clerk, Lord Strathnairn and others of high and distinguished positions at home and in India. A lady knight also adds a peculiar grace to the order, in the person of the loyal and able Secunder Begum of Bhopal. So popular and esteemed has the Star of India become, that a second and third class of the order have since been added, to be worn by those who have rendered distinguished service to the State, in military or civil capacities in India, but whose rank and position are not sufficient to place them on an equality with the original knights of the order.

CHAPTER XIII.

MILITARY.

From the first moment of his taking office to the last day before his retirement, the affairs of the army, in one shape or another, caused Sir Charles Wood more anxiety and exhausting labour than any other subject that came before him.

The year 1859 has been well described as being "the year of India's suspense." The mutiny was crushed, the protracted sieges and reliefs, the hard-fought battles, the dearly-won victories, were all over. Tantia Topee, the last of the rebel chiefs, had been treacherously betrayed by his own followers, and had expiated his crimes on the gallows; but, though the work of the soldier in the field was concluded, the whole question of the future constitution of our armies in India remained to be considered.

While the rebellion of the mutinous sepoys had come to be looked upon as a thing of the past, another danger little anticipated, and at the time much underrated, arose.

In the Bill introduced into Parliament by Lord Stanley for the transfer of the powers and possessions of the East India Company to the Crown, their

European troops had been transferred also, without a passing allusion to them, or to their new position. The transfer was, in fact, purely nominal; they had been the servants of the Company as the trustees of the Crown, they became the servants of the Crown without the intervention of the Company; but every right and every privilege which they had enjoyed as soldiers of the Company were scrupulously secured to them as soldiers of the Crown.

The men, however, tempted perhaps by an opportunity of obtaining their discharge, and a renewed bounty on re-enlistment, or perhaps by the fancy of a visit to England, strenuously, and even mutinously, opposed their transfer to the direct service of the Crown. This was the first of the many difficulties which met Sir Charles Wood on his accession to office.

It is important to notice at this time what was the actual position of the European portion of the Indian army.

Up to 1852 the European troops consisted of two regiments of infantry in each presidency; in that year a third regiment was added; and during the mutiny an additional force of European soldiers was raised, and the officers of the new artillery, cavalry, and infantry, were taken from those of the native artillery and native regiments which had disappeared or been disbanded.

In the year 1858, a Royal Commission was appointed to inquire into the reorganization of the Indian army. On the question whether the European forces in that country should be exclusively Royal artillery and cavalry, and infantry of the line, or partly of this description, and partly a local force, the Commission were nearly equally divided—the members of it connected with the Indian services being in favour of a local service,—the other members being opposed to such a system. They reported, however, in favour of an exclusively line army. Lord Stanley, however, decided, against the report of the Commissioners, that the European forces in India should be partly local and partly general.

Upon Sir Charles Wood becoming Secretary of State for India, the European troops in the service of the East India Company amounted to 24,000, being in excess of the numbers authorized by law to be maintained by them. It was necessary, therefore, that an Act should be passed, legalizing this excess.

In introducing a Bill for that purpose into Parliament, Sir Charles Wood had announced his determination to abide by the decision of his predecessors in office, and to maintain a local army for India.

The mutinous conduct of the European troops, however, convinced Lord Palmerston's Government that it was not expedient to maintain in the Queen's army a body of European troops exclusively for service in India, and other reasons, indeed, led to the same conclusions.

The disclosures made during the inquiries into the late disaffection of the European troops, had converted Sir Hugh Rose, Sir William Mansfield, and Sir Patrick

Grant, from being advocates of the local force, into supporters of a contrary system.

The discipline of the old Indian army was confessedly and notoriously inferior to that of the Queen's troops, and it was acknowledged that long service in a tropical climate deteriorated troops in that respect as well as others. Lord Clyde urged that it was "absolutely necessary not to trust to local "corps, but to put faith alone in a discipline which is "constantly renovated by return to England, and the "presence of officers with their regiments who look "on these as their homes."

In June, 1860, therefore, Sir Charles Wood introduced into the House of Commons his proposal for the reorganization of the Indian army, in a Bill entitled "The European Forces Bill."

The difficulty of this question, great enough in itself, was increased by the opposition of the Council of India, whose members fondly clung to the recollection of the old service with which they had been associated, and in which some of them, perhaps, had passed some of their happiest days.

They urged on financial grounds, that, as India paid for the whole of her military expenditure, none of the troops should be liable at any time to be withdrawn for Colonial or European purposes. On the same grounds it was argued that the expense of a Royal army far exceeded that of a local force. The proposals of the Government were further opposed, on the grounds of acclimatization being necessary for the troops employed in India, the impolicy of placing more authority in the hands of the Horse Guards, and the difficulties of checking patronage and expenditure.

The soundness of these arguments was very questionable.

The matter was one of such a character, that it had to be looked at from an Imperial rather than from a departmental point of view. It was very carefully considered, therefore, by Lord Palmerston's Government, and it was ultimately determined by them to discontinue the local European troops, and to provide for the whole of the European force to be stationed in India, by increasing the artillery, cavalry, and infantry of the line, in the Queen's general army.

All the European troops in India were to be relieved periodically, as those regiments of cavalry and infantry had been, which for many years had formed the largest portion of the European force in India.

It was not to be expected that this measure, as to the expediency of which the opinions of the great authorities in India materially differed, would pass unchallenged in the House of Commons. Lord Stanley and Sir De Lacy Evans both spoke in favour of the maintenance of a local force; but the opposition in Parliament was not sufficient to defeat the measure, which was passed by large majorities; and the amalgamation, or more properly the conversion of the European troops of the Indian army into troops for general service, was finally adopted.

The European soldiers of the East India Company

had the option of volunteering for the Queen's service, and with few exceptions both officers and men availed themselves of the offer, the latter receiving a small bounty. Fourteen brigades of artillery, three regiments of cavalry, and nine regiments of infantry, were added to the establishment of the Queen's regular forces, and this part of the army question was thus satisfactorily brought to a close.

The insubordination of the European troops, however, was not the only difficulty that had to be overcome.

The native army in India consisted, before the mutiny, of seventy-four regular regiments in Bengal, fifty-two in Madras, and thirty in Bombay. The number of officers attached to each infantry regiment was twenty-six, to each cavalry regiment twenty-four; but, according to the invariable practice, a certain portion, not exceeding seven, of these officers was withdrawn from their regiments for service in other ways. Besides these troops, there were irregular regiments, with only three European officers, and these were generally admitted to be the *corps d'élite* of the whole army.

The regular army had, as far as Bengal was concerned, almost ceased to exist; for, whereas before the outbreak of the mutiny there were eighty-four regiments, cavalry and infantry, in 1859 only seventeen were left, though the officers of all the original regiments remained. In Madras, the former number of regiments still existed, and in Bombay there had been only a small diminution of numbers; so that, including the new levies embodied during the mutiny, the whole army in India amounted to 260,000.

It was indispensable to take into serious consideration the question of what was to be done with the native army. The danger of an overgrown native force, the pressure upon the finances and on the maintenance of so large a number of men, the prospects of peace, all pointed alike to reduction. But, beyond the diminution of numbers, it was thought expedient, partly with a view to improve the character of the regiments, partly from considerations of expense, to change the organization of the army, and to adopt the system which had worked so successfully in what were called the irregular regiments, with a smaller number of picked officers, receiving higher allowances. That the effects of this reorganization were advantageous to the native officers and soldiers was never disputed; but the question as to the European officers of the native army was different altogether. The diminution of force naturally led to a diminished number of officers, and the change in the organization of the army rendered the reduction still larger. A considerable number of officers thus became supernumerary.

Had such a reduction taken place in the British army, the difficulty would have been met by placing all supernumeraries on the half-pay list; but such had not been hitherto the practice of the Indian Government. The fact was, that ever since our possession of India, our territories, and consequently our armies, had always been on the increase; so that only once since the East India Company existed had any reduction, and that a very small one, taken place. It is obvious that no question could be more difficult of solution than one in which the personal claims and personal interests of so many officers were concerned. Nothing daunted, however, Sir Charles Wood encountered the Herculean task, which has proved not less difficult than he anticipated, and has lasted to the end of his administration, with all its technical details, all its grievances—some real, some imaginary, but none that were intentional, and none which, when proved, it has not been sought to redress, by the incessant care and attention of those to whom the execution of details was entrusted, and by labour almost incredible.

If Sir Charles Wood experienced opposition from the Council in originating and proposing these great measures, he met with their cordial and hearty support in carrying them out.

It had been a frequent subject of complaint that the efficiency of the old local European and native regiments was most seriously affected by the large number of officers, and those the most capable, being withdrawn from service with their regiments for staff employment. Under the term "staff" employment were included appointments in all branches of public works, telegraph, surveys, engineering, ordnance, political, commissariat, stud, and pay departments, besides the general staff of the army. Those that were so taken for civil employment became naturally unaccustomed to their military duties, and, what is perhaps of more importance, they lost their interest in the men of their regiments, were unknown and without influence with their brother officers and their soldiers, while those that were not so favoured were inclined to be discontented and dissatisfied, aiming not so much at military proficiency, and an acquaintance with their men and their regimental duties, as at future employment in places of superior emolument and greater interest.

It had been a subject of frequent discussion during the existence of the late East India Company, how to meet this crying evil and to provide officers for the various situations in which their services were required, without impairing the efficiency of the regiments.

The only scheme which afforded the means of attaining so desirable an end, was the formation of a Staff Corps, which had been frequently recommended by high authorities, including such men as Sir John Lawrence, Lord Elphinstone, Sir Bartle Frere, Sir Herbert Edwardes, and Sir Patrick Grant, the last of whom expressed his hope that under this system the European officers would look upon their regiments as their homes. "To be attached," he wrote, "to a native corps would be considered one "of the prizes of the service; and the permanent "association between officers and men that must "ensue, would more than anything tend to restore "the old feeling of mutual respect and attachment "which, in the early days of British power in India, "united the native soldier and his European officer." The institution of a staff corps was also recommended by a committee presided over by Lord Hotham, which sat for the purpose of considering the measures to be adopted for the amalgamation of the Indian forces.

Besides the improved efficiency of the army anticipated from such a change, the financial part of the question was well worthy of consideration. A sum, it was calculated, of 330,000*l.* per annum would be saved to the revenues of India by the change.

It was determined, therefore, to organize a Staff Corps to which both Indian and Queen's officers might be appointed, but which would be ultimately filled up by candidates selected from the Queen's general service; while those officers of the Indian forces who had not been transferred to the Queen's army or joined the Staff Corps, would be employed as heretofore with native regiments, or in various situations on the staff.

On the 16th of January, 1861, Sir Charles Wood advised the issue of a royal warrant, authorizing the formation of a staff corps to provide officers for general employment, as well as for regiments which had been placed on the irregular system.

One of the chief difficulties attendant upon the new order of things, was to devise the best system of promotion for the officers in the staff corps. The fluctuation of the number as the necessity for more or less officers was felt, prevented the adoption of any scheme but that of length of service; and indeed, Lord Hotham's committee had recommended "promotion in the staff "corps to be governed by length of service, and to be "irrespective of departmental position."

The option of joining this corps was given to all officers of the Indian army who were in staff employment, or who had been so within a certain time, and the benefit of counting towards promotion, time previously served in such employment, as if it had been in the staff corps, was accorded to those officers who entered it on its formation.

Upwards of 1,300 officers availed themselves of this privilege, which, in very many cases, gave additional promotion, as well as additional pay.

This liberality on the part of the Government led to complaints from those who, remaining in the position of regimental officers only, were thus liable to a supersession in army rank. Sufficient precautions were taken to prevent their being superseded in regimental duties.

These complaints were pressed upon Sir Charles Wood, who, with every anxiety to remedy any reasonable grievance, appointed, in 1863, a commission, presided over by Lord Cranworth, and comprising Lord Ellenborough, Lord Hotham, and Mr. Henley (the mover of the original parliamentary clause, guaranteeing to the officers of the old Indian armies, all those " advantages as to pay, pensions, " allowances, privileges, promotion, and otherwise," which they would have enjoyed, had they continued in the service of the East India Company), as well as Sir Charles Yorke, General Clarke, and Sir Peter Melvill, " to inquire into and examine whether any " departure from the assurances given by Parliament " had taken place by reason of the measures which " have been taken since the passing of the first- " mentioned Act for the better government of India, " by the Secretary of State in Council, or by the

"Government or military authorities in India, towards such reorganization and amalgamation as aforesaid."

This commission made their report in November, 1863, having classed and arranged the various complaints they had received from officers under thirteen heads, the principal of which were the following :—

1. Retention on cadres of names of officers transferred to the staff corps.

2. Retention on the cadres of European regiments of the names of officers who joined the representative line regiments.

3. Injury to the remaining officers, from the greater healthiness of service in the staff corps.

4. Or in representative regiments.

5. Retardation in attaining colonel's allowances in ordnance corps.

6. Injury to officers as regards funds for retirement.

7. Discontinuance of Indian allowances to regimental colonels residing in India.

8. Cancelling an order for ante-dating commissions in ordnance corps.

On three points the commissioners considered that the parliamentary guarantee had been infringed; the first being the immediate and prospective supersession in rank of regimental officers, by those in the staff corps, which was the inevitable consequence of the rule regulating promotion in the staff corps, and especially of that which allowed previous staff service to count towards the period of service qualifying for promotion in the staff corps.

Measures were at once adopted for remedying this complaint, on its being pronounced by the commissioners to be well founded; and it was decided to give brevet rank to the regimental officers of the Indian army, and local rank to the officers of the line serving in India, from the formation of the staff corps, so that from that date the whole of the officers of the Indian army, including the staff corps, will be promoted in army rank after the same periods of service. Sir Hugh Rose, now Lord Strathnairn, with all his affection for the officers of the Indian army, with whom his name is so nobly associated, recorded his opinion that these measures adequately met the complaint of supersession, and the Government of India declared that all substantial ground of complaint was removed.

The two other points were—the retention, on the cadres of native corps, of the names of officers who joined the new line regiments, and the arrangements for the future promotion of officers of the Indian army to the rank of general officers.

To obviate the first of these two complaints, Sir Charles Wood directed that the names of all officers who have joined the new line regiments from the native cavalry and infantry should be removed from the cadres, and that promotion should take place in the vacancies so caused.

To remedy the second, the provisions of the royal warrant, regulating the future amalgamation of the field officers of the British and Indian armies, were modified, so as to retain the whole of the officers of the cavalry and infantry of the Indian army, on the general list of that service as before, for promotion to the rank of general officers.

Thus were the three points in which the parliamentary guarantee was reported to have been infringed dealt with in a generous and comprehensive spirit.

There were two complaints on which the Royal Commission expressed no positive opinion.

These were :—

1st. The regulation by which twelve years is made the period of service in the grade of lieutenant-colonel, for the attainment of colonel's allowances.

2nd. The reduction of the regimental lieutenant-colonels by making promotion in succession to one-half only of the officers of that rank, who accepted the special annuities offered to them on retirement in 1861.

The period of twelve years was adopted, on what was considered as a fair calculation, being somewhat more than the time recently taken to pass through the colonels' grade in Bengal and Bombay, but less than that in Madras; and this term was so fixed absolutely, only in respect to the officers who attained the rank of lieutenant-colonel after the 1st of January, 1862, and whose promotion to that rank had been accelerated by the liberal scheme of retirement.

The officers who were lieutenant-colonels before 1862 have attained to the colonels' allowance under the previously existing rules, unless, as was the case with many officers of the Madras army, the new rule was more favourable to them.

With regard to the second complaint, that the

number of lieutenant-colonels was reduced by promotion in succession to one-half only of the retirements in 1861, it must not be forgotten that these retirements were the result of an extraordinary measure, involving considerable expense, which gave special annuities to a larger number of officers, who were thereby induced to retire.

It was impossible to contend that the guarantee could have been intended to prevent the Crown, if, in the interest of India and of the empire at large, it should deem it necessary, from reducing the number of the Indian army. And, when the native army was reduced by 135,000 men, it could not with justice be made a matter of complaint that the number of colonels' allowances should be gradually diminished. The Government, on the reduction, did not place a single officer on half-pay; and, with the exception of this diminution of colonels' allowances, they continued their full allowance, as well as promotion, to those officers for whom, owing to the various circumstances mentioned above, there was no employment.

Lord Cranworth's commission had reported that, if it was impossible to retain all the advantages enjoyed under the East India Company, some counterbalancing benefit should be given in compensation for them.

It would be too long a task to explain in detail all the advantages accumulated upon officers by the measures of the Government. A few examples will show that they were many and great.

The immediate effect, in a pecuniary sense, was to increase the pay, pensions, and emoluments, in one shape or another, of the existing officers, by more than a quarter of a million sterling.

A glance at the number of promotions to substantive rank in the three Indian armies in the four years ending January, 1857, and the four years ending January, 1865, will show how the promotions have increased. In the latter period there were 233 promotions to the rank of lieutenant-colonel, against eighty-four in the former; to that of major there were 534 against 142; and to the grade of captain, 616 against 585, or against 409, if 176, which were due to augmentation, be withdrawn from the calculation.

These advantages were with great fulness demonstrated to the House of Commons, by Sir Charles Wood, in a debate brought on by Captain Jervis; but, unfortunately for the encouragement of an agitation damaging to the discipline of the army, on a division in a thin House, an address was carried praying the Crown to "redress all such grievances complained of "by the officers of the late Indian army as were "admitted by the commission on the memorials of "officers to have arisen by a departure from the "assurance given by Parliament."

Another commission was thereupon issued for the purpose of inquiring into the effect of the measures already adopted with this object.

This commission having only to deal with questions affecting pay and promotion, was composed entirely of officers of the army. General Sir John Aitchison acted as chairman, and it rested with them, according to the instructions they had received, to report whether the brevet rank given to all officers of the Indian army effectually removed the cause of the complaint that regimental officers might, in certain contingencies, be superseded in rank and command by officers of the staff corps; whether any retardation of promotion which might hereafter take place in a few cases, from not filling up all the vacancies caused by the extraordinary retirements, and fixing twelve years as the term of service in the rank of lieutenant-colonel, consequent on the great reduction of the army, is to be considered as a departure from the parliamentary guarantee; and, if so, whether the increased pay, pensions, and general acceleration of promotion conferred on officers, are not an adequate counterbalancing benefit.

It was in the autumn of 1865 that the commissioners made their report, pointing out where the measures taken fell short of what was required for removing the causes of complaint, or for giving such counterbalancing benefit in lieu thereof. Their report received from Sir Charles Wood immediate and constant attention, but his accident and subsequent resignation of office prevented his completing the task he had undertaken. The question was left to his successor Lord de Grey, and it was well that Lord Russell's choice fell on one whose previous official career had been exclusively connected either with India, as Under Secretary, or with the English army, as Under Secretary and Secretary of State for the War Department. Conversant as he thus had become with all military matters, and assisted by Mr. Stansfeld as his under secretary, and the military members of the council, he at once gave his best consideration to the settlement of the matter. Indeed a despatch was actually prepared under his directions, but not signed, when Lord Russell's administration resigned office.

Lord de Grey did not consider himself justified in settling so important a matter on the eve of his retirement, but left his opinions and his despatch to his successor, who shortly after, in the House of Commons, enunciated the measures to be adopted by the Government for the remedy of the alleged grievances of the officers of the Indian army.

He adopted entirely the conclusions which had been arrived at by his predecessor in office with regard to all the points touched on in the report of Sir John Aitchison's commission. All officers belonging to that army before the amalgamation, were to be allowed to join the Staff Corps without any condition or test whatsoever.

And further, Lord Cranborne issued instructions to the Government of India, for compensating, to some extent, the officers who could prove that they had not received an equivalent advantage for the sums which they had from time to time contributed, for purchasing out their regimental superiors.

Every one who has the interests of the Indian army at heart, will wish that this long-vexed question may now for ever be set at rest, and will join with the present Secretary of State in hoping, "that all who " have taken up the case will use their influence to do " all they can to put a stop to a system of agitation, "most mischievous to the Indian service, and most inconsistent with the ordinary attitude which officers ought to assume towards the Government."

If the measures adopted for the amalgamation of the army did not give the satisfaction that they ought to have done to individuals who were too apt to consider, not whether they themselves had been fairly dealt with, but whether others had not, amidst many necessary changes, been more fortunate than they, it is consoling to find that there were other military changes during this period on which there can be little or no difference of opinion.

In 1863 sanitary commissions were nominated in each Presidency, in accordance with the recommendation of a sanitary commission appointed in 1859 to inquire into the best means of selecting the sites of military stations, improving the health, and preventing epidemic and other diseases incidental to the British soldier serving in India.

Sir Hugh Rose's noble efforts for the amelioration of the condition of the soldier in the East were at all times cordially approved and seconded at home.

Workshops, as well as gardens, gymnasia, fives-courts, baths, cricket-grounds, skittle-alleys, refreshment-rooms, have all been instituted to relieve the soldier from the depression and lassitude of an enervating climate ; additional pay was given ; the period of service entitling them to good-conduct pay was reduced ; the odious order of 1836 instituting "half batta" for all troops within 200 miles of presidency towns, in consequence of the supposed facility with which they obtained supplies from England, was withdrawn, and full batta granted to all soldiers, wherever stationed.

In 1864 fifty good-service pensions were announced for officers of distinguished and meritorious service, and a capitation allowance was granted to all effective members of Volunteer Corps.

All these benefits could not be given without a corresponding charge on the revenues; but the additional outlay will not be considered ill spent, if it should be proved that there is a compensation in the shape of increased health and comfort, and prolonged life, to the soldier, and new popularity to a service on which much of our prosperity and safety in India depends.

CHAPTER XIV.

POLICE.

THE subject of the reform of the police in India engrossed much of Sir Charles Wood's attention. The military character it had assumed, and its increased numbers, had entailed enormous charges on the Indian revenues.

"Hordes of military police and local levies, whose "name was legion," said an article in the *Calcutta Review* of June, 1861, "and whose aggregate nume-"rical strength has probably never been accurately "known to any one, had grown up in every district, "pervaded every town, and patrolled every highway, "and bid fair, if allowed to remain undisturbed, to "become as great a source of anxiety in the future as "the pretorian Sepoys had proved in the past, while "for the time being they consumed the revenue of "the country."

There were many systems, no one like another, and no uniformity of plan or discipline. In Madras alone a purely civil force had been organized, responsible only to an inspector-general, who was to be in direct communication with the Government. It was impossible, however, having in view the many requirements of various districts, to dispense altogether with an armed police throughout India, but it was advisable to define more clearly the duties of the civil and military forces.

In July, 1860, an able and exhaustive memorandum, embodying the views of Sir Charles Wood on the principles on which a police force was to be organized throughout India, was sent to the several presidencies of Bengal, Madras, and Bombay,

Lord Canning, seeing at once the pressing nature of the subject, appointed a police commission, its members being carefully selected from men of experience from all parts of the country.

In consequence of the unanimous report of that commission, Act V. of 1861 was passed in the Legislative Council of India, and a civil constabulary is now introduced in all the presidencies, their duties being to preserve tranquillity in ordinary times, to protect life and property, and to perform many duties heretofore discharged by sepoys, such as furnishing guards for escort of bullion, for gaols, for public treasuries, &c.

An improved police has enabled Government not only largely to reduce the number of native troops, but has to an incalculable extent restored discipline to regiments who, under the old system, were constantly broken up and scattered on detached duties, considered by all military men to be eminently subversive of proper regimental control and discipline.

The supervision of the police is henceforward to be intrusted to European officers, themselves responsible to a chief appointed directly for that purpose, and subordinate only to the local Governments.

The new system, from the trial that has already been made of it, holds out every prospect that it will prove really efficient and far superior to the old and effete system which it has supplanted. "We believe," said an Indian writer, " the wheels of police adminis- " tration have now got into the right groove, and we " look with confidence to the experience of the next " ten years to bear us out in our conclusions, and to " justify our hopes."

Sir Charles Wood was also desirous of seeing vigorous and effective measures taken for the improvement of the village watch, who were to be carefully selected, and to be placed under proper and sufficient superintendence, under the control of the magistrate.

No great reform in the village watch could well be carried out without the co-operation and assistance of the heads of the villages, the landholders, and local chiefs. Sir Charles Wood was anxious to follow up, throughout India, the judicious course pursued by Lord Canning in Oude and the Punjab, and to invest the Native country gentlemen with considerable magisterial and executive powers; and he impressed upon the Government of India the value of enlisting the influence of the landed proprietors in favour of the public interests, not only by law, but by the steady pursuit, on the part of the magistrates, of such conciliatory measures as should lead them to consider themselves as parties concerned in the general administration of the country, rather than as servants of the district authorities.

CHAPTER XV.

NAVY.

IN the beginning of 1860 great uneasiness prevailed among many thinking men in India, on account of the insufficiency of the naval defences of our British possessions in the Indian Seas; the Indian Navy, gallant as her officers and able as her seamen had proved themselves, was of course utterly unable to cope with the overwhelming forces that any large European power might bring against it, and many years and many millions of money would hardly serve to put it in a position capable of defending our Eastern Empire. Indeed, even for the purposes for which it was intended, of suppressing piracy and slave trade in the Persian Gulf and Indian Ocean, its condition was far from satisfactory; many of the larger and most expensive ships were almost useless for any service, were under-officered and under-manned, and the uncertainty of its future as a fighting navy had affected all classes and seriously impaired its former efficiency. " Its extinction was most desirable," wrote Lord Canning; " it is a service extravagant " to the state, disheartening to the officers, and " utterly inefficient, owing to its nature, not to the "fault of officers or men." It was necessary that some remedy should be devised for this state of affairs, and the subject had to be regarded by Sir Charles Wood from an European as well as an Indian point of view. He decided upon its abolition as a fighting service, retaining only a sufficient number of vessels for purposes of surveying, transport, &c. In the first instance the number of ships in commission was reduced as far as practicable, and those that were not absolutely required, were directed to be sold; it was not therefore till 1863 that the abolition of the Indian navy was actually accomplished.

No appreciable dissatisfaction at the measures adopted has been created; officers of all ranks and grades have been pensioned on a liberal scale, and the local Governments directed, in all cases when it is possible, to employ the officers of the late Indian navy, where suitable opportunities present themselves, the men being discharged gradually, and with due regard to the demand for their services in the mercantile marine. The defence of the seaboard of India is now altogether intrusted to the Royal Navy, and the Cape of Good Hope command is extended to the East Indies, with the addition of a commodore, whose head quarters are at Bombay.

The wisdom of this arrangement is very evident, remedying as it does all the objections raised against the insufficiency of Indian Naval defence, while the enormous expenditure which would have been required to place the existing navy in a proper fighting position, has been obviated.

Much correspondence with the various offices at home has taken place respecting the transport of Indian reliefs and their passage through Egypt, instead of the long sea voyage round the Cape of Good Hope. After considerable discussion, and notwithstanding some objections, it has been determined that the service shall commence in the autumn of 1867, by which time five first-class steam transports, it is expected, will be completed, and ready for service. This means of transport will be much more economical than the old service round the Cape, and will, naturally, be far more rapid and advantageous to the discipline of the troops, which is always apt to deteriorate in long sea passages. The service will only be conducted during those months which are adapted in a sanitary point of view for the passage and landing of the troops in India.

CHAPTER XVI.

CONCLUSION.

It was in the autumn of 1865 that Sir Charles Wood had an accident in the hunting-field, which, though exaggerated at the time, was nevertheless so severe as to compel him, in the beginning of the following year, to resign his office of Secretary of State for India to a younger colleague in the Cabinet, anxious to continue the liberal policy developed in his predecessor's administration.

It was impossible that Sir Charles Wood could have witnessed, without some feelings of pride and satisfaction, the sincere regret caused by his retirement from the field of Indian politics. To him, the enforced relinquishment of a life's pursuit must inevitably have been a source of much regret. To those associated with him in official business it was a matter of deep sorrow, and at the council-table, when he announced his retirement, there were few who could trust their voices to express the emotion which they felt. Though Sir Charles Wood had frequently differed with individual councillors, his masterly conduct of business, his quick appreciation of merit, his experience and knowledge, his frank manners, and his liberal consideration for the feelings and opinions of others, had won a place in every heart, and those who had differed from him the most, were not those who regretted his loss the least.

Nor was it only with those who personally knew him that this feeling existed. The native princes of India, the wealthy merchants of Bombay, the talookdars of Oude, the poor and needy ryots of Bengal,—all vied with each other in the expression of their regret. " The native press knew well to
" whom was due the credit of the successful and bene-
" ficent administration of India," which, to quote the words of the address of the British and Indian Association, " has nobly sustained the authority and dignity of
" her Majesty's Government in her Indian territories;
" which has strengthened by new bonds of attachment
" the confidence and sympathy of the princes and
" chiefs of the country, which has, above all, steadily
" sought to govern the empire in consonance with
" justice and the true interests of her teeming millions.
" Indeed, from one end to the other, the country rings
" with the praises of Sir Charles Wood. We might
" have, but for his too rigid justice and impartiality,
" been cursed by the European adventurer, whose
" claims to superior privileges by reason of colour and
" creed he would not admit; but he has the blessings,
" spontaneous and sincere, of two hundred millions of
" fellow-creatures, whose good he has sought with a
" single-minded zeal. If the conscious satisfaction of
" having discharged his duty and advanced the cause

" of humanity and justice constitute the best and
" richest reward which a statesman can reap in this
" world, Sir Charles Wood has that reward. May he
" reign over us for all the time God may be pleased
" to spare him to serve his fellow-men."

THE END.

LONDON:
PRINTED BY SMITH, ALDER AND CO.,
OLD BAILEY, E.C.

NEW WORKS
PUBLISHED BY
SMITH, ELDER AND CO.

Turkey and the Crimean War. By Rear-Admiral Sir Adolphus Slade, K.C.B. Demy 8vo.

Life and Speeches of Lord Plunket. With a Preface by Lord Brougham, and a Portrait. Edited by the Hon. David Plunket. 2 vols. Demy 8vo.

A Manual of Marine Insurance. By Manley Hopkins, Author of "A Handbook of Average," &c. Demy 8vo.

The Sporting Rifle and its Projectiles. By Lieut. James Forsyth, Bengal Staff Corps. Second Edition, Re-written and Enlarged. With Illustrations. Crown 8vo. 7s. 6d.

A Century of Painters of the English School. With Critical Notices of their Works, and an Account of the Progress of Art in England. By Richard Redgrave, R.A., (Surveyor of Her Majesty's Pictures, and Inspector-General for Art,) and Samuel Redgrave. Two vols. Demy 8vo. 32s.

Life of Michael Angelo. By Herman Grimm. Translated by F. E. Bunnett. With Photographic Portrait from the Picture in the Vatican. Second Edition. Two vols. Post 8vo. 24s.

Raphael: His Life and His Works. By Alfred Baron Von Wolzogen. Translated by F. E. Bunnett. With Photographic Portrait. Crown 8vo. 9s.

The Life and Death of Jeanne d'Arc, called "The Maid." By Harriet Parr. With Portrait. Two vols. Crown 8vo. 16s.

In the Silver Age. By Harriet Parr. With Frontispiece. Crown 8vo. 6s.

** Library Edition in Two Volumes, Crown 8vo. With Two Illustrations, price 12s.

The Life of Goethe. By George Henry Lewes. New Edition, partly Re-written. One vol. 8vo. With Portrait. 16s.

Aristotle; a Chapter from the History of Science. With Analyses of Aristotle's Scientific Writings. By George Henry Lewes. Demy 8vo. 15s.

William Hogarth; Painter, Engraver, and Philosopher. Essays on the Man, the Work, and the Time. By George Augustus Sala. With Illustrations. Crown 8vo. 7s. 6d.

LONDON : SMITH, ELDER AND CO., 65, CORNHILL.

WORKS ON
INDIA AND THE EAST.

Christianity in India. An Historical Narrative. By John William Kaye. Demy 8vo. 16s.

*The Life and Correspondence of Major-*General Sir John Malcolm, G.C.B., late Envoy to Persia, and Governor of Bombay. From Unpublished Letters and Journals. By John William Kaye. With Portrait. Two vols. Demy 8vo. 36s.

The Life and Correspondence of Charles, Lord Metcalfe. By John William Kaye. A New and Revised Edition. With Portrait. Two vols. Post 8vo. 12s.

Selections from the Papers of Lord Metcalfe, late Governor-General of India, Governor of Jamaica, and Governor-General of Canada. By John William Kaye. Demy 8vo. 16s.

A History of Persia, from the Beginning of the Nineteenth Century to the year 1858. With a Review of the Principal Events that led to the establishment of the Kajar Dynasty. By Robert Grant Watson, formerly attached to her Majesty's Legation at the Court of Persia. Demy 8vo. 15s.

Journal of a Diplomate's Three Years' Residence in Persia. By E. B. Eastwick, Esq., late H.M.'s Chargé d'Affaires at the Court of Tehran. Two vols. Post 8vo. 18s.

*Journal of a Political Mission to Afghani-*stan, in 1857. With an Account of the Country and People. By H. W. Bellew, Medical Officer to the Mission. With Eight Plates. Demy 8vo. 16s.

Reminiscences of a Bengal Civilian. By William Edwards, Esq., Judge of Her Majesty's High Court of Agra. Crown 8vo. 7s. 6d.

The Englishwoman in India. Containing Information for the Use of Ladies proceeding to, or residing in, the East Indies, on the Subject of their Outfit, Furniture, House-keeping, the Rearing of Children, Duties and Wages of Servants, Management of the Stables, and Arrangements for Travelling, to which are added Receipts for Indian Cookery. By a Lady Resident. Second Edition. Crown 8vo. 6s.

Works on India and the East. 3

Farming in India, Considered as a Pursuit
for European Settlers of a Superior Class. With Plans for the construction of Tanks, Dams, Weirs, and Sluices. By Lieutenant-Colonel Greenaway, of the Madras Staff Corps. Post 8vo. 5s.

The Bhilsa Topes; or Buddhist Monuments
of Central India; Comprising a Brief Historical Sketch of the Rise, Progress, and Decline of Buddhism. By Major-General Alexander Cunningham, Bengal Engineers. With Thirty-three plates. Demy 8vo. 30s.

Egypt, Nubia, and Ethiopia. Illustrated by One Hundred Stereoscopic Photographs; with Descriptions and Numerous Wood Engravings. By Joseph Bonomi, F.R.S.L., and Notes by Samuel Sharpe. Small 4to. Elegantly bound. 3l. 3s.

Idylls from the Sanskrit. By Ralph T. H. Griffith, M.A., Principal of the Sanskrit College, Benares. Fcap. 4to. Cloth, gilt edges. 10s. 6d.

The Rifle in Cashmere. A Narrative of Shooting Expeditions in Ladak, Cashmere, &c. With Advice on Travelling, Shooting, and Stalking. By Arthur Brinckman, late of H.M.'s 94th Regiment. With Two Illustrations. Post 8vo. 3s. 6d.

The Wild Sports of India; with Detailed Instructions for the Sportsman; to which are added Remarks on the Breeding and Rearing of Horses, and the Formation of Light Irregular Cavalry. By Lieutenant-Colonel Shakespear, late Commandant Nagpore Irregular Force. With Portrait of the Author. Second Edition, much Enlarged. Post 8vo. 5s.

Stanzas by a Century of Poets; being Japanese Lyrical Odes. Now first Translated into English, with Explanatory Notes. The Text in Japanese and Roman characters, and a full Index. By F. V. Dickins, M.B. Demy 8vo., cloth, gilt edges. 10s. 6d.

The East Indian Ready Reckoner. A Series of Tables, showing the Cost of any Number of Articles, in Indian Currency, from 1 pie to 1 rupee, advancing 1 pie at a time. Including Numbers answering to Fixed Indian Weights and Measures. By C. D. Demy 8vo. 6s.

Indian Exchange Tables. In Two Parts. Part I.—Converting Sterling Money into East India Company's Currency. Part II.—Converting East India Company's Currency into Sterling Money. Calculated from 1s. 8d. to 2s. 4d. per rupee, progressing by Eighths of a Penny. By J. Henry Roberts. Second Edition. Revised and Enlarged. Demy 8vo. 10s. 6d.

A Digest of Moohummudan Law on the Subjects to which it is usually applied by British Courts of Justice in India. Compiled and Translated from Authorities in the Original Arabic. By Neil B. E. Baillie. Demy 8vo. 28s.

LONDON: SMITH, ELDER & CO., 65, CORNHILL.

WORKS BY MR. RUSKIN.

Modern Painters. Complete in Five Volumes.
Imperial 8vo. With Eighty-seven Engravings on Steel, and Two Hundred and Sixteen on Wood, chiefly from Drawings by the Author. With Index to the whole Work. 8*l.* 6*s.* 6*d.*

      ·Each Volume may be had Separately.
  Vol. I. Of General Principles and of Truth. 18*s.*
  Vol. II. Of the Imaginative and Theoretic Faculties. 10*s.* 6*d.*
  Vol. III. Of Many Things. With 18 Illustrations on Steel. 1*l.* 18*s.*
  Vol. IV. On Mountain Beauty. With 35 Illustrations on Steel, and 116 Woodcuts. 2*l.* 10*s.*
  Vol. V. Of Leaf Beauty; of Cloud Beauty; of Ideas of Relation. With 34 Engravings on Steel, and 100 on Wood. With Index to the Five Volumes. 2*l.* 10*s.*

The Stones of Venice. Complete in Three Volumes, Imperial 8vo. With Fifty-three Plates and numerous Woodcuts, drawn by the Author.

     Each Volume may be had Separately.
  Vol. I. The Foundations. With Twenty-one Plates. 42*s.*
  Vol. II. The Sea Stories. With Twenty Plates. 42*s.*
  Vol. III. The Fall. With Twelve Plates. 31*s.* 6*d.*

The Seven Lamps of Architecture. With Fourteen Plates drawn by the Author. Second Edition. Imp. 8vo. 21*s.*

The Crown of Wild Olive: Three Lectures on Work, Traffic, and War. Second Edition. Fcap. 8vo.; gilt edges, 5*s.*

The Ethics of the Dust: Ten Lectures to Little Housewives on the Elements of Crystallization. Crown 8vo. 5*s.*

Sesame and Lilies; Two Lectures. I. Of Kings' Treasuries. II. Of Queens' Gardens. Third Edition. Fcap. 8vo. Cloth, gilt edges. 3*s.* 6*d.*

Lectures on Architecture and Painting. With Fourteen Cuts. Second Edition. Crown 8vo. 8*s.* 6*d.*

The Elements of Drawing. With Illustrations. Seventh Thousand. Crown 8vo. 7*s.* 6*d.*

The Elements of Perspective. With Eighty Diagrams. Crown 8vo. 3*s.* 6*d.*

The Two Paths: Being Lectures on Art, and its Relation to Manufactures and Decoration. With Two Steel Engravings. Crown 8vo. 7*s.* 6*d.*

  LONDON : SMITH, ELDER & CO., 65, CORNHILL.

www.ingramcontent.com/pod-product-compliance
Lightning Source LLC
Chambersburg PA
CBHW020844160426
43192CB00007B/780